BLAIRSVILLE SENIOR HIGH SCHOOL
BLAIRSVILLE, PENNA.

DISCRIMINATION

JEWISH AMERICANS STRUGGLE FOR EQUALITY

DISCRIMINATION

JEWISH AMERICANS STRUGGLE FOR EQUALITY

by
GEOFFREY BAR-LEV
and
JOYCE SAKKAL

Rourke Corporation, Inc.
Vero Beach, Florida 32964

Cover design: David Hundley

∞ The paper used in this book conforms to the American
National Standard for Permanence of Paper for Printed
Library Materials, Z39.48-1984.

Library of Congress Cataloging-in-Publication Data
Bar-Lev, Geoffrey, 1948-
    Jewish Americans struggle for equality / by Geoffrey
Bar-Lev and Joyce Sakkal.
        p.   cm. — (Discrimination)
    Includes bibliographical references and index.
    Summary: Discusses the struggle of Jews to secure
equal rights in the United States.
    ISBN 0-86593-182-8 (alk. paper)
    1. Antisemitism — United States — History — Juvenile
literature.   2. Jews — United States — History — Juvenile
literature.   3. United States — Ethnic relations —
Juvenile literature.   [1. Antisemitism — History.   2.
Jews — United States — History.   3. Ethnic relations.]
    I. Sakkal, Joyce, 1964-   . II. Title.   III. Series.
DS146.U6B37   1992   92-7473
305.892'4073 — dc20   CIP
                                                  AC

CONTENTS

DISCRIMINATION

JEWISH AMERICANS STRUGGLE FOR EQUALITY

1 What Is Discrimination?

Prejudice and discrimination have persisted since the beginning of humankind despite efforts to contain them. To understand better the causes of prejudice, the social sciences such as history, economics, sociology, and psychology offer penetrating insights. Through these tools, one can learn much about the deep origins of hatred and find out what can be done to prevent or change these widespread feelings.

Historically, deep-seated conflicts such as religious ones between Christianity and Judaism and racial ones between blacks and whites have provided humankind with targets for the release of hostility and feelings of hatred. These prejudicial feelings are often transmitted from generation to generation by parents and the societies in which people grow up. This heritage can be seen today in people's inability to explain logically their hostility toward certain groups: They hate or dislike all or most members of a group but are unable to explain rationally why.

To avoid falling victim to such thinking, one must develop the capacity to recognize discrimination and prejudice and build the sophistication to combat them. Through education and reason, one can gain the confidence needed to question the legitimacy of traditional prejudicial attitudes and develop the courage to confront intimidating social pressures, which often force people to accept unfounded prejudice as truth. Yet, even education is not always sufficient to eliminate prejudice, as the record of history amply demonstrates. Education must be combined with a strong sense of justice and respect for others.

Discrimination and Prejudice

Prejudice and discrimination are closely related notions, but they are not one and the same and therefore require separate definitions. Discrimination has often been distinguished from prejudice as being a behavior, an overt and organized practice that actively applies and reinforces prejudiced thinking, while prejudice has been defined as an attitude, a passive way of seeing things. The poison of prejudice generally afflicts larger population numbers than discrimination does, but not all those who are prejudiced discriminate. To discriminate, one must have social, economic, or political power.

Discrimination can be defined as the practice of categorical and unfavorable exclusion or restriction of a group on the basis of race, gender, religion, or nationality. Discrimination can also be targeted against other groups of people, including the young, the old, the poor, the rich, the handicapped, the mentally ill, the diseased, and the homosexual.

Prejudice, on the other hand, is an emotional attitude that involves both prejudgment and misjudgment of people. It is an "irrational attitude of hostility directed against an individual, a group, a race, or their supposed characteristics," as Webster's defines it. Those who are prejudiced not only select facts that fit within their prejudgments and stereotypes, thus misinterpreting the facts, but also staunchly attempt to defend and rationalize their distorted perceptions.

Two Age-Old Problems

Prejudice and discrimination are not uniquely modern-day problems but ancient and universal ones. Human beings have

German soldiers shaving the beard of a Jewish man; victims of prejudice are seen by their persecutors as less than human. (Library of Congress)

always had a tendency to hate those who are different. This has sometimes resulted in the destruction of past civilizations such as the Incas of South America and the North American Indians. The spoils went to the victor, the losers were usually slaughtered, and the survivors were subjugated to second-class citizenship. In Montevideo, Uruguay, a magnificent sculpture towers in memory to the nation's extinct Indian population.

In modern times, intergroup hatred became common in nations composed of people of different races, nationalities, and religious backgrounds. In the past, such societies were formed through wars of conquests, when different peoples were forced to live together. Examples of such societies can be seen in Northern Ireland, the civil war in Yugoslavia, and the breakup of the Soviet Union. In recent times, specifically in industrial, democratic states, culturally diverse societies are usually formed through waves of immigration. This is particularly true of the United States, where millions of immigrants have come from every part of the world.

Discrimination In the American Colonies

The first British settlers to arrive in the Colonies in the 1600's and 1700's were Protestant groups fleeing religious persecution in Europe. Among the cultural baggage they brought with them was the concept of British "pure blood" and a belief in superiority of the white race. This racist ideology set the basis for justifying the dehumanizing institution of slavery and the shameful treatment of Indians.

The Indians and the blacks, however, were not the only groups persecuted in the Colonies. Others were too, but to a much lesser extent. Americans of English origin, forgetting their own history, turned persecutors themselves. When Jews, Italians, Eastern Europeans, and other immigrants arrived, they were sometimes met with hostility and bigotry.

In the nineteenth century, when 1.5 million Irish fled the potato blight in Ireland, they disembarked on American soil only to face another kind of hardship: anti-Catholicism and anti-immigrant sentiments. Americans thought that Irish slums were tarnishing the prosperous image of the nation, decreasing the value of the land, and disgracing the American people. They also feared the threat that unskilled Irish workers posed to the job security of Americans. As a result, thousands of Irish suffered great social and economic deprivation. "No Irish Need Apply" signs reflected dominant feelings and left countless Irish workers unable to support themselves or their families. The nineteenth century also witnessed the flourishing of anti-Semitic ideas, blaming American problems on a conspiracy of international Jewry and paving the way for the establishment of several anti-Semitic movements in the twentieth century.

Because many of the immigrants were poor and thus willing to work for any wage, they were seen as economic rivals, a threat to be confronted. Whether they were poor or successful, immigrants were blamed for every imaginable social and economic problem: The Germans were resented for their success in farming; the Irish Catholics were blamed for everything from alcohol abuse to economic upheavals. Efforts to fight these prejudices resulted in increased tensions.

Progress and Change in American Attitudes

Today, many people in the United States are still victims of prejudice and discrimination because of their race, their nationality, their religion, or some other factor that makes them different from the majority. They may be recent immigrants from Korea or Vietnam, migrant workers from Mexico, or people who have some kind of physical disability.

However, despite the continuing rejection and harrassment of certain groups, substantial progress has been made in the past few decades to improve intergroup relations. Efforts undertaken by the Supreme Court in the rulings of the 1940's and 1950's, the U.S. Congress' Civil Rights bills of the 1950's and 1960's, the activities of powerful organizations, and continuous protest movements have all been effective strategies in reducing discrimination. Their calls for ending discrimination have been joined by numerous other groups and private individuals in a rallying cry for justice, humanity, and the upholding of democratic values.

Causes of Prejudice and Discrimination

Many causes exist for prejudice and discrimination, but prejudice constitutes the first and major explanation of how discrimination begins. It is significant to note that the recipients of hatred are not usually responsible for any of those causes. Instead, it is the persecutors, shaped by their environment, who fabricate negative images of their scapegoats. Their attitudes reveal more about themselves and their shortcomings than about their victims.

The Parental Factor

One of the earliest ways prejudice can form is by subconscious imitation. During a child's first few years, parents have a tremendous influence on the development and shaping of their child's attitudes and emotions. Not only are children extremely impressionable, but also they like to mimic. They hear derogatory terms such as "niggers," "chinks," "kikes," and they innocently repeat them. They hear that these people are lazy or those people are troublemakers, and such stereotypes leave imprints on their mind. Displays of emotions, such as irritability, gestures, and tone of voice, add validity to their impressions, which are further reinforced by family members, friends, and the community environment. Because children see their parents as being all-knowing, responsible adults, they assume in good faith that their parents are correct in their perceptions. Therefore, children pick up their parents' stereotypes and become prejudiced themselves without knowing how and why. Often, the parental influence continues into their child's teenage years and even into adulthood.

Prejudice as Tradition

Such a family environment can explain another cause of prejudice: conformity to traditional prejudicial attitudes. This is especially true of close-knit groups who avoid intermingling with members of other groups, especially the ones against whom they hold a prejudice. Such people live in ethnic communities, having contact mostly with people of their own background.

Reinforced by frequent repetition, group prejudices develop and discourage individuals from forming relationships with people from other groups. To do so would weaken the cohesiveness of the group, challenge the validity of its traditional values, and weaken the controlling power of the dominant members. In some cultures, severe punishment or expulsion from the group was used to punish those who did not conform. Because of peoples' need to belong, most conform to the belief system of the group. As a result, bridging contacts between groups are limited, and distrust is increased.

Prejudice as a Product of Anger

Another way prejudice can form is through what psychologists call projection or displaced resentment. When people are angry, frustrated, and disappointed with themselves or their situation, they feel the need to release their frustrations. Some do so by blaming their problems and failures on others, instead of confronting themselves, which is much harder to do. The feeling of power and superiority they gain by finding fault with others provides temporary relief from the pain and embarrassment of their own weakness.

Such people are often angry at authority figures, such as parents, teachers, or employers. Their culture, however, has taught them to respect their superiors. They are thus prohibited from venting their anger at them. Feelings of resentment grow, and they create scapegoats, approved by society, as targets on whom they can take out their frustrations.

Whatever the motive, whether it is fear, anger, jealousy, or ignorance, prejudice almost always satisfies an emotional need. People who are prejudiced do not form an opinion through knowledge, good judgment, or reason; instead, their views are dominated by uncontrolled and unexamined feelings.

Consequences of Prejudice and Discrimination

The effects of prejudice and discrimination are so devastating that they cannot be measured. In terms of emotional scars and ruined hopes, the poison that hatred afflicts on men, women, and children can cripple their lives forever. Discrimination produces feelings of inferiority, worthlessness, and outrage, among many others. Whenever people are made to feel that way, they will want to hurt back in defense or to get even. This backlash can result in delinquency, vandalism, crime, as well as a life behind bars.

By choosing to make the United States their home, Americans of all origins have chosen to follow the path of freedom, democracy, and equality. They have chosen a society based on those principles, whose population represents the world within a nation. The people of the United States make a mosaic of cultures that enrich all of our lives. Successful interactions with so many people from diverse backgrounds undoubtedly requires an open and curious mind.

2 The Historical Roots of Anti-Semitism

The term "anti-Semitism" was introduced in Germany during the 1870's to describe negative attitudes toward people born into the Jewish faith. The word "Semitic" refers to a race of people who inhabited the Middle East region four thousand years ago. The Semites are believed to have originated in the deserts of what is present-day Saudi Arabia and then infiltrated the Middle East through ancient Mesopotamia or Southern Iraq of today. Today's Arabs are the descendants of the Semitic peoples.

Originally known as the Hibaru, the Hebrews, who were the first to develop Judaism, were also Semites. In the biblical account of their history, they are known as the Israelites. The confusion over their name can be understood if one keeps in mind that the Hebrews were a collection of tribes belonging to the Semitic race. Hebrew was and is their language. Judaism is their religion, and Israel is their country and national identity. Anti-Semitism refers to prejudice and the resulting persecution directed against the Hebrews and their descendants from antiquity to the present.

Today known collectively as Jews, the Hebrews have been singled out for their religion since their beginnings. Also persecuted for their race and as a nation, they have been mainly resented for their adherence to Judaism. Because of their tenacity and conviction in their faith, they have never been destroyed, surviving all of their conquerors over the past three thousand years.

Centuries of Persecutions and Invasions

In the pre-Christian era, the Hebrews created a small nation situated at the crossroads of the world where they were invaded repeatedly by great empires. They survived the Egyptian captivity, when Moses led the children of Israel in an unprecedented escape out of slavery. They survived the Assyrians, the Babylonian exile, and the onslaught of ancient Greece. They were finally defeated by the Roman Empire and expelled from Israel. As stateless people for 1,800 years, the Hebrews were persecuted by Christians and Muslims alike. Their situation went up and down, determined by changing attitudes toward them in the countries in which they lived. With the spread of democratic movements in the nineteenth century, some European states voted them equal rights as citizens, yet in the twentieth century anti-Semitism became more virulent than ever, culminating in the Holocaust.

The Hebrews have been the most persecuted people in the history of humankind. No other race, religious group, or nation has been the recipient of such a fierce and enduring hatred. Since the time of the biblical Abraham, who is said to be the first Jew, their history has been filled with unspeakable crimes committed against them. The Hebrews have been the object of hatred in pagan, religious, and secular societies. They have been resented when rich and beaten when poor. They have been accused of being communists, and communists have branded them capitalists. Millions of people have believed — and some still do — that Jews want to control the world, that they caused plagues and murdered Christ, the son of God.

Jews Introduce Monotheism to a Pagan World

The Hebrews of antiquity were the first monotheists — that is, the first people in the world to believe in one God. They also believed that as guardians, they were chosen to carry this message to the rest of humanity. At a time when most people believed in many gods, Jewish beliefs conflicted greatly with those of their neighbors. The Hebrews angered surrounding tribes because Judaism totally rejected pagan idols. In those days, tribes honored each others' gods as a common courtesy in intertribal dealings. In this clash, which set the pattern for many subsequent conflicts, the Hebrews saw themselves as upholding higher values but were seen by their neighbors as being antisocial.

Uncommon Jewish practices further aroused pagan suspicions. The Israelites' stress on circumcision, symbolizing membership in an elect nation, was generally seen as barbarous. Dietary and cleanliness laws, which kept the Hebrews apart, contrasted with the emerging Greek view of the oneness of humanity. The observance of the Sabbath, a revolutionary practice at the time, also differentiated the Israelites from other people. In antiquity, the fact that Jews were very different was the origin of anti-Semitism.

However, as advanced as the Hebrews were spiritually, they retained many backward superstitions and were not on the leading edge in technology nor culture. The Hebrews sought to maintain a distinct identity in part because they themselves periodically fell under the influence of their neighbors and slipped back into idol worship. Separation was not only a preventive measure, but also it was designed to protect their beliefs and traditions against overwhelming forces that were bent on destroying them.

Early Fabrications of Negative Images of Jews

In the three hundred years before Christ, many anti-Semitic writings appeared as a result of the clash with Greco-Roman culture known as Hellenism. The most damaging is known as the Ur-Libel. Manetho, a Greek-speaking Egyptian priest, wrote in

Anti-Semitic images from Germany, showing Jews as ridiculous yet diabolical; note the emphasis on Jews as killers of Christ. (Library of Congress)

250 B.C. that Moses was not a Hebrew but a rebellious Egyptian priest who led a revolt of outcasts, lepers, and negroes. The Ur-Libel was widely believed and became the foundation of all future anti-Semitism. It was meant to discredit the Hebrews, Israel, and Judaism.

Slanders and inventions against the Hebrews were fabricated partially in response to the feelings of superiority the Hebrews felt in their monotheism. That Jews worshiped donkeys, conducted human sacrifices, and were more likely to contract leprosy were common lies. The Israelites' refusal to worship the Roman Emperor branded them disloyal troublemakers. Greek intellectuals inspired official Roman hostility with anti-Semitic propaganda and poisoned the minds of rulers.

The Hebrews were driven out of Israel after two failed revolts, in A.D. 66-70 and A.D. 132-135, in which at least half a million Jews were put to the sword by Roman legions. Thousands upon thousands of Hebrews were sold into slavery, while Jewish gladiators were favorites in Roman arenas. The surviving population scattered throughout the Mediterranean area.

During those last years before their defeat, the Hebrews were deeply affected by centuries of occupation, first by the Greeks and then by the Romans. Every Israelite institution, especially the synagogue, struggled to survive under extreme pressure to accept the Greco-Roman worldview. In desperation, the Hebrews sometimes turned to radical leaders and religious fervor was common. Many claimed to be the Messiah coming in time to save Israel. When they became troublesome, they were routinely turned over to the Romans by the Israelite puppet government. It was during this period that Jesus of Nazareth lived.

The Controversy Over the Death of Jesus

Of all the layers of anti-Semitism, the accusation that the Jews killed Christ has caused Jews the most pain and suffering. The circumstances leading to the trial of Jesus in a Jewish court and the resulting crucifixion by the Romans make up a minefield of deep controversy between Christians and Jews, still unresolved today. Because there is little precise information about the events surrounding the death and the status of Jesus, the matter is open to interpretation and is a question of faith.

The known facts remain, however, that the original disciples were all Jews who believed in Jesus, his theology, and his criticisms of the synagogue at the time. Jesus himself was a Jew, well trained in Jewish laws, whose intent was to reform Judaism. At his trial, Jesus knew very well that by standing silent he was inviting the death penalty. After his death, the Jews who believed in his resurrection may be called the first Christians. It was the belief in the resurrection that separated the Jews who believed in Jesus from traditional Jews. Christianity, the religion, came later.

In the third century A.D., Jewish Christians and traditional Jews became opponents. With the beginning of the Church in the fourth century A.D., pagan anti-Semitism was infused with new Christian anti-Semitism. The Jews were thought to be carrying collective responsibility for the death of Jesus. It was widely believed that all their future generations were to pay the price for Jesus' death, with conversion to Christianity their only hope for salvation. Christendom saw itself as the new Israel, and the Jews were seen as rejecting the will of God. As more and more pagans accepted Christianity, the Jews were excluded from society and slipped into centuries of powerlessness.

After the fall of Rome, while Europe entered a period of cultural decline known as the Dark Ages, a new religion was born in what is today Saudi Arabia. Led by Mohammed, their prophet, the Arabs were united, conquering vast territory and converting the population to Islam. When the Jews of Medina refused to accept Mohammed as their prophet, he ordered all males beheaded publicly. Thus, not only in Europe but also in the Middle East and throughout the Islamic world, the Jews were seen as rejecting the one who was believed to be the true prophet.

Religion and Superstition as Sources of Hatred

For centuries, the Jews were at the mercy of leaders who were willing to protect them from a superstitious population molded by Church-sponsored anti-Semitism. An example of this occurred during the period of the Crusades, when whole Jewish communities were massacred in their homes in England by Christian mobs. The "blood libel," a widely believed lie that Jews kidnaped and killed young Christian boys to reenact the killing of Jesus, fueled the mobs. Whenever such charges were investigated, the Jewish defendants were found not guilty. Soon, it was discovered that because Jews were in the business of lending money and charging interest, which was banned by the Church at that time, they were vulnerable to such allegations.

When the bubonic plague swept through Europe in the thirteenth century, killing nearly half the population, the Jews were the first to be suspected. Under torture, some "confessed" to spreading the disease by poisoning wells to get back at Christians. Pope Clement VI had to remind the populace that the Jews were suffering from the plague as much as anyone else. Many popes throughout the history of the church, however, were not sympathetic to Jews, scheming to convert them by any means. Some of the most celebrated saints in Catholicism were dedicated anti-Semites responsible for the deaths and torture of thousands of Jews.

In 1492, the Spanish monarchs Ferdinand and Isabella began enforcing religious policies that became known as the Spanish Inquisition. Hundreds of thousands of Christians were punished for alleged religious transgressions. Under the threat of death, Jews were forced to convert to Christianity; afterward, they were sought out for allegedly practicing Judaism secretly. Some twenty thousand "secret Jews" were legally burned alive. The Spanish Inquisition succeeded in expelling almost all Spain's 200,000 Jews in what was a new form of government-sponsored anti-Semitism.

Martin Luther, the founder of the Protestant branch of Christianity, also tried to gain the support of the Jews for his new interpretation of the Bible. Amazed when they would not convert to his Christianity, he turned against them with a fury. Luther urged that synagogues be set on fire, Jewish prayer books be destroyed, and rabbis be forbidden to preach. Then their homes were to be destroyed, their property seized, and the Jewish population drafted into forced labor. In the ensuing inter-Christian struggle known as the Reformation and Counter-Reformation, Jews were persecuted and victimized by both Catholics and Protestants.

The Ten Commandments, part of the rich Jewish legacy to the moral and religious traditions of Western civilization. (Bill Aron/PhotoEdit)

Jewish Contributions Engender Suspicion

For most of the 1,800 years that the Jews lived in foreign lands, they were limited to occupations allowed to them. Though some Jews rose to positions of high privilege, their power was usually short-lived and sometimes ended in tragedy and disaster. Under more favorable rulers, the Jews became educated and contributed greatly to medicine, map-making, business, law, and various desirable skills.

Often more skilled and better educated than Christians, these elite Jews were needed by rulers and tolerated by the Church. The majority of Jews, however, were forced to eke out a living as middlemen in the midst of a hostile population. Pitted against Christians, Jews came under scrutiny for their business practices. Already considered untrustworthy because they were not Christians, they were generally not trusted in commerce. Though some Jews undoubtedly took advantage of some Christians, the majority were honest. Nevertheless, the Jew was seen as self-serving, greedy, and unscrupulous. The tenacious myth of the dishonest, greedy Jew has survived until this day.

Political Anti-Semitism and the Holocaust

As the pace of change accelerated in Western societies, the "Jewish problem" remained a constant irritant in Christian Europe. Throughout the Enlightenment, the most prominent writers, such as Voltaire, attacked Judaism and tried to discredit it. With the emergence of democracies, religious anti-Semitism simply carried over to political anti-Semitism. The Industrial Revolution created opportunities for Jews but at the same time caused rivalry between Christians and Jews, strengthening political anti-Semitism. Rising nationalism further isolated Jewish minorities in almost every country in which they lived, the United States being an exception. The myth about Jewish dual loyalty, that Jews were not trusted patriots in the countries in which they lived, arose at this time adding another layer to modern anti-Semitism.

It was against this backdrop of rapid change, of new ideas and old hatreds, that the greatest of all the tragedies of humankind took place. During the reign of the Nazis in Germany, the persecution of Jews became legal through the Nuremberg Laws of 1935. Under those laws, Jews were forced out of the mainstream of society and were slowly impoverished. Their property was seized and their synagogues were burned. In the Nazi view, the Jew was seen as a member of the most inferior race, clinging to a false faith and yet intelligent enough and powerful enough to control the world. This contradictory view, combined with centuries of condoned anti-Semitism, made it possible for brainwashed Germans and others to participate in, or ignore, the systematic mass murder of Hebrews during the Holocaust.

In antiquity, the Hebrews were the great innovators in religion and morals. During the Dark Ages, they were teachers transmitting sacred knowledge. They slipped into obscurity, to be seen as backward people deluded by a false faith. Then, at the end of the eighteenth century, they broke out and transformed human thinking once again. The Jews were not only innovators but truth-tellers, as they saw it, dramatizing and clarifying the human condition. Maybe it is because of their role of being at the center of controversy throughout history that they have been hated so much.

3 The Jewish American Experience

After the discovery of the New World by Christopher Columbus in 1492, some of the first people to settle in North America were Christians escaping persecution by their fellow Christians in Europe. New Christian ideas and beliefs, inspired by the Protestant Reformation, challenged the Catholic Church and traditional Christian tenets. The resulting religious strife in Europe led some to risk the long and dangerous journey across the Atlantic Ocean to live at the edge of the wilderness in the New World.

The Puritans, a Protestant sect, began arriving in North America in the early 1600's, believing that they were to purify Christianity of European corruption and establish a new Christendom in the New World. Moreover, the Puritans identified with the first Jewish Christians of antiquity. They saw themselves as true Jews, and they interpreted their experience in terms of biblical parallels. They compared their escape from Europe to the escape of the children of Israel, the ancient Jewish people, from slavery in Egypt. Furthermore, just as Moses led the children of Israel to the Promised Land, so the Puritans saw America as their Promised Land, their "New Jerusalem." Yet, while they were obsessed by such parallels, the Puritans did not like Jews or Judaism. They had brought anti-Semitic baggage with them from the old country.

Traditional Jewish culture placed a high value on study. (P. Cantor/Uniphoto)

The Beginnings of Jewish Immigration

Few Jews came to the New World during the initial stages of settlement. Not only discouraged by the dangerous journey, most Jews could not imagine living in the wilderness completely isolated from European Jewry and the urban skills to which they were adapted. Those who came to America at first were Jews who were least bound to Judaism and the Jewish community. In the thirteen original Colonies, the Jewish population numbered only some 250 persons in 1700, and 2,000 out of three million Americans at the time of the Revolution in 1776. Synagogues existed in Charleston, New York, and Philadelphia in colonial times, but it is estimated that one out of every four of these early Jewish immigrants left Judaism, either because of intermarriage or because of isolation in remote areas far from the very small Jewish community.

The history of the Jews in North America began in 1654, when twenty-three Jewish refugees arrived in New Amsterdam

(New York) to an inhospitable welcome by the Dutch governor
Peter Stuyvesant. Unfavorable toward Jews, the governor was
reluctant to let the refugees stay. His fear that a Jewish
community might arise in New Amsterdam required
consideration by his superiors at the Dutch West India Company
in Holland. Pressured by wealthy Jews in Amsterdam who had
significant investments in the Dutch West India Company, the
Dutch were persuaded into allowing the Jewish refugees to stay in
New Amsterdam. The status of the Jews as citizens and their
right to practice Judaism openly became hotly debated issues, but
in practice, these issues were irrelevant as more and more Jews
arrived. The Jews came to New Amsterdam to trade. If they
succeeded, despite anti-Semitism, there was nothing to stop them
from worshiping in their own way in the New World.

After the British expelled the Dutch from North America in
1664, all the residents of the Colonies became British subjects.
Under English law, however, Jews did not have political equality
in any of the thirteen Colonies. They could not vote in elections
for representatives to colonial legislatures. Since the Jews had no
such rights in England, they should not have such rights in the
New World, it was argued. While American Christians did not
regard Jews as their equals, as the only non-Christian settlers, the
Jews generally encountered less prejudice than Catholics.

Economic Freedom and Jewish Contributions

The vital issue for the Jews, however, was economic freedom.
Their experience in Europe had taught the stateless Jews that
through success in commerce they could acquire some degree of
influence and security in a society hostile to them. In America,
Jews enjoyed equal rights in commerce, if not in politics. Indeed,
Jewish businessmen were highly regarded and respected for their
honor and uprightness. In America, as nowhere else, Jews were
free to choose any occupation they pleased. Ultimately, the
colonies were economic entities needing people willing to work

and make something of themselves, whether they were Jews or
not. By the outbreak of the American Revolution in 1776, nearly
half the population of the Colonies belonged to religious sects
such as the Quakers and other groups outside the Protestant
mainstream. The Jews in America were not the only group that
was different.

For their small number, American Jews did contribute greatly
to the American Revolution, though there were too few Jews in
the Colonies to influence significantly the character or the
outcome of the Revolution. Figures such as Haym Salomon
helped prevent the Continental Congress from going bankrupt by
advancing the newly established American government $200,000
in hard currency needed to provision the armies. Jewish civilian
ship owners financed some of America's first naval warships. The
importance of Jews in America during the Revolution was not in
what they did but in the fact that they were there at a crucial
time. The awareness that not all the citizens of the United States
of America were Christians led to laws idealizing equal rights for
all people under the new Constitution.

During the Revolution and the founding of the Republic, there
was no discussion of the Jews. However, the antireligious views
of the European Enlightenment spread to America, bringing with
them criticism of Jews and Judaism as well as Christianity. The
ideas that Jews were of a perverse race, that Christianity was a
false religion, that Gentiles should free themselves from
superstitious Christianity and turn to the "God of Reason" were
given voice in America by Thomas Paine. Though the Protestant
majority detested Paine's antireligious philosophy, they more or
less agreed with his anti-Semitism. However, the equality of the
Jews under the law was never questioned. Jews were white;
therefore, they were never subjected to the prejudice that
American blacks were forced to endure. By 1820, Jews were
generally accepted, though most Christians believed that Jews
should abandon their religion and assimilate.

Jewish Population Growth, United States, 1790–1990

Year	Number
1790[b]	1,200
1818[a]	3,000
1826	6,000
1840	15,000
1848	50,000
1880	230,000
1888	400,000
1897	938,000
1900	1,058,000
1907[b]	1,777,000
1917	3,389,000
1927	4,228,000
1937	4,771,000
1950[c]	5,000,000
1960	5,531,000
1970	5,870,000
1975	5,732,000
1979	5,860,900
1990	5,981,000

[a]Estimates for 1818–1899 are based on "Jewish Statistics," AJYB, Vol. 1, 1990, p. 623.

[b]Estimates for 1790 and 1907–1937 are from Nathan Goldberg, "The Jewish Population in the United States," *The Jewish People, Past and Present,* Vol. 2 (New York, 1955), p. 25.

[c]The 1950–1979 estimates are taken from AJYB, Vols. 70–80, 1969–1980.

The small population of some six thousand mostly American-born Jews was increased to 150,000 by the arrival of a massive wave of Jewish immigrants in the mid-nineteenth century. As in colonial times, the Jews who came to North America in the middle of the nineteenth century were nearly all poor and uneducated. About half of these Jewish immigrants came from Germany, while many came from other places in Central Europe. At a time when America was booming with economic prosperity and westward expansion, the Jews brought with them their

experience in buying and selling. Fortunes were amassed by
Jewish immigrants who started in business by selling from carts
in the streets of the larger cities. Not forgetting European
persecution, by 1850, the Jews entered American politics to help
their brothers and sisters worldwide, though America was not yet
a major player on the international stage.

The Civil War and Anti-Semitism

On the eve of the Civil War, the Gentile majority in the United
States, who knew little or nothing about Jewish beliefs and
practices, regarded the Jews as different. It was noted, though,
that Jewish merchants drove themselves harder than Gentiles and
became successful quicker. The fact that Jews denied the divinity
of Jesus, the fundamental belief of all Christian groups in
America, was also noted. The Jews, however, wanted to become
Americans accepted by the society at large. The celebrated and
controversial Isaac Mayer Wise waged a vigorous fight against
anti-Semitism, particularly against the Christian teachings that
blamed Jews for the crucifixion. Wise wanted to see an America
where the Protestant majority had no special privilege.

During the Civil War, American Jews also could not avoid
becoming embroiled in the issues of slavery and states rights.
Jews residing in the South generally supported the Confederacy,
while Jews living in the North preferred to preserve the Union.
Southern Jewish clergy unanimously endorsed the seceding
states. Northern Jews, fearing the disruption of commerce, hoped
for a gradual solution.

The Civil War stimulated anti-Semitism on both sides of the
Mason-Dixon line. In 1862, Ulysses S. Grant, then commander in
Tennessee, expelled all Jews from territory under his jurisdiction.
Because of anti-Semitism, Jews were unfairly singled out as
major culprits in the profitable smuggling trade across battle
lines. Condoned by both sides, smuggling was a way through
which the North could get cotton while the South acquired

A Hanukkah lamp from the nineteenth century, a period of large-scale Jewish immigration to the United States. (Smithsonian Institution)

needed tobacco and finished goods. A resolution to repeal the order was introduced in Congress but failed in both houses. President Abraham Lincoln himself revoked the order.

In the five decades after the Civil War, the period that saw the heaviest immigration in American history, approximately two million of the thirty-five million newcomers were Jews. Flight from anti-Semitic violence and poverty were the major reasons for immigration. America gave refuge to Jews escaping pogroms in Czarist Russia and severe persecution in Eastern Europe. In America, the law was not their enemy. There were some Americans who wanted to enact legislation restricting immigration. The proponents of such legislaion were usually racists who preferred immigrants from Northern and Western European stock. However, American business and industry generally opposed such laws, needing cheap immigrant labor. Most people believed that the children of the immigrants would become upstanding Americans.

Life was difficult for most Jewish immigrants at the turn of the century. Attracted to some half-dozen large American cities, Jewish immigrants poured into ghettos such as the Lower East Side in New York City. Having to toil long hours in sweatshops for meager wages, their children took to the streets, shining shoes, selling newspapers, or doing anything to help the family make ends meet. Jewish prostitutes were a majority in New York for a time. Juvenile gangs roamed the streets stealing from pushcarts, while gambling became a pervasive recreation for adults. Many young Jewish men turned to sports as a quick road to success. At one point in the 1920's, seven of the nine boxing titles were held by Jews. Jews also became prominent in the emerging silent films era of Hollywood. Whatever their field of endeavor, these children of the Jewish ghetto believed that they could make their way into American society only by acquiring power.

Two World Wars and Immigration Policies

During the years of World War I and the postwar period, American Jewry tested its power in an unsuccessful battle against a widely supported but biased American immigration policy. Those in favor of restricting immigration invoked supposedly "scholarly studies" as "proof" of the lower mental and moral nature of Jews, Slavs, and Italians. The fact that Jews participated at the highest level in the Russian Revolution of 1917 and the Communist labor movement in the United States added another reason for limiting Jewish immigration. The most famous American industrialist, Henry Ford, financed a newspaper that spoke for American anti-Semitism in the 1920's. Though there was little violence against Jews in the United States, they were quietly excluded from banking, finance, and the management of heavy industries such as steel, coal, and automobile manufacturing. In the 1930's, quotas were set in colleges, universities, and medical schools restricting the number of Jewish students. After the stock market crash of 1929, American anti-Semitism rose as a result of economic hardship, especially in the Farm Belt, where there was also a devastating drought that turned the soil into dust.

With the advent of Adolf Hitler's Nazism, more than 200,000 Jewish refugees were admitted to the United States between 1933, when Hitler took over Germany, and the end of 1941. Mostly middle-class and educated, these arrivals were different from their predecessors. Some of those who came were celebrated scholars, artists, ranking scientists, and social thinkers who were at the pinnacle of intellectual life in Europe. Personages such as Albert Einstein, Marc Chagall, and others were looked upon as enlightened teachers, but the morale of Jews was lower than ever. The news from Europe was shattering, yet immigration quotas were filled or blocked by Washington. Powerless American Jewry had no choice but to watch the unfolding of an unbelievable tragedy in Europe.

At the same time, Jews were visible at the upper levels of the administration of President Franklin Delano Roosevelt. Some of Roosevelt's most trusted advisors were Jews, and Henry Morgenthau, Jr. was secretary of the treasury. A master politician, Roosevelt manipulated American Jewry, who saw him as their protector and almost unanimously supported him at the polls. Through Felix Frankfurter (who helped shape the policies of the New Deal before Roosevelt appointed him to the Supreme Court in 1939), the Jewish figure closest to Roosevelt, Jewish leaders raised their deep concerns for European Jews and the stringent immigration laws in the United States preventing rescue. Though Roosevelt became more and more sympathetic to the

Bar Mitzvah boy holding Torah in front of ark. (Gregory Teitelbaum)

plight of European Jewry, he could not be so publicly. Introducing Jewish issues to an anti-Semitic and isolationist United States would have hindered Roosevelt's plans to prepare Americans gradually for World War II.

After the war, when the full extent of Nazi crimes was revealed to the world, American public opinion quickly turned around in support of Jews. The fighting Jews of Palestine inspired American imagination. The fact that the Jews were battling not only the Arabs but also the British appealed to Americans. The state of Israel may never have been created in 1948 if it were not for American public opinion supporting the idea of a Jewish homeland.

Bar Mitzvah boy reading from the Torah during the sabbath service. (Gregory Teitelbaum)

Jewish Americans in the Postwar Years

During the economic expansion of the postwar era, like most Americans, American Jews basked in the new prosperity that quickly changed the face of the entire nation. Jews also joined in the rush to the suburbs, buying homes and sometimes invading areas restricted to them. A new Americanism espoused by President Dwight D. Eisenhower pronounced all religions dedicated to the United States as good. The reason for this philosophy was to gain support of all peoples for the United States' struggle against the Soviet Union and Communism, which threatened the American way of life and the United States' vision for the world. Helped by this environment, Jewish Americans participated enthusiastically in those dreamy years and became wealthy enough to exercise their power on the United States for the first time.

With the election of John F. Kennedy as President in 1960, American Jewry entered a new era of political power in the United States. Their years of loyalty to the Democratic Party had been rewarded. In the 1960's, Jewish businesses and careers were almost unobstructed, and Jewish-American students attended the finest universities. Anti-Semitism was no longer troublesome, while Israel's overwhelming victory in the 1967 war infused the American Jewish community with pride and confidence. The Vietnam War, however, loomed in the background, deeply dividing the nation. Anti-war demonstrations and riots in black ghettos shook the United States. The black-Jewish alliance ended after Israel's victory, and some Christian churches withdrew their support for Israel, forcing American Jews to reexamine their position in the United States. The continuing deterioration of relations between the United States and Israel under the administration of President George Bush became a matter of deep concern to American Jews, who have not forgotten their bitter history in Europe.

4 Decades of Discrimination

Jews in the American past were occasional victims of informal discrimination in the social, political, economic, and academic arena. Anti-Jewish ideologies and restrictions against Jews were never sanctioned by legal establishments and governmental policies, but they were present in many influential circles, camouflaged under a complexity of motives. The mere existence of such motives and their widespread support reflected the ambivalences and traditional anti-Jewish prejudices felt by large segments of American society.

The Distinct Case of Anti-Semitism

Some historians have argued that anti-Semitism was a European phenomenon with little influence in America, and that any hostility Jews encountered on American soil was simply the rejection of one more immigrant group by native-born white Americans. At first, this contention sounds plausible, considering all the immigrant groups, besides Jews, who were subjected to rejection. However, it fails to recognize the uniqueness of historical Jewish-Gentile relations and deep-seated hatred of Jews, embodied in the folkloric picture of Jews as Christ-killers and stigmatized in the greedy and dishonest image of Shylock, the unyielding moneylender in William Shakespeare's *The Merchant of Venice*. The cumulative effects of centuries of persecution, indoctrination, and negative representation of Jews were not going to disappear following an ocean voyage across the Atlantic. Thus, it is not surprising that Old World suspicions and enmity were transplanted to the New World and were to a certain extent retained, distinguishing the peculiar nature of anti-Semitism from the experience of other immigrant groups.

The American Colonies and the Jews

In the early period of the American Colonies, stereotyped notions about negative Jewish traits were mild and were not promoted by any particular group. Jews were absorbed in American society with relative ease and without too many incidents of overt discrimination for two reasons: First, the Jewish population was still relatively small; second, the presence of so many dissenting and oppressed immigrants and the freedoms flowing from the American Revolution and the Constitution helped discourage the growth of anti-Semitism.

Nevertheless, Jews in the Colonies found themselves surrounded mostly by Europeans who, in their flight from European persecution, saw America as a sanctuary for oppressed Protestants. In an attempt to protect themselves and their newfound homeland, European-Americans tried to impose limitations on undesirables, no matter how large or small their numbers were. These limitations were not present in all the Colonies, but wherever present, their victims included deists, atheists, non-professing Christians, and Catholics as well as Jews, who often found themselves objects of prejudice and discrimination.

Of all the colonies, New Amsterdam in the mid-1650's made Jews feel the most unwelcome. Under the governorship of Peter Stuyvesant, Jews were at first denied economic and religious freedom. Attempts were made to exclude them from military service, to prevent them from engaging in commerce, and to forbid them from worshipping in public. The transition from Dutch rule to a more tolerant British rule in 1664, when England occupied New Netherland, improved the situation of the Jews, but they had to struggle hard for their rights to compete in business, worship in public, and hold office.

In another manifestation of colonial anti-Semitism, John Russell, a British statesman with influence over colonial affairs, voiced his opposition in 1753 to the "Jew Bill" and the naturalization of Jews born on foreign soil, as well as to the Naturalization Act of 1740, which applied to the Colonies. Russell not only claimed that both bills would flood England with Jews and would discourage Protestant settlements in America but also feared a Jewish plot to control Christians in both England and America and thus protested their right to vote and own land.

Throughout the 1700's, a number of pastors and missionaries expressed their anti-Jewish prejudices in their preachings. In 1768, an Anglican missionary by the name of John Beach rejoiced at the situation of the Jews, the dissolution of their state, and their exile. Repeating a popular theme, Beach insisted that as long as Jews did not recognize Jesus they would continue to suffer.

Anti-Jewish incidents elsewhere in the Colonies under both Dutch and British rule could be seen in unfair lawsuits, arrest, and fines; slanderous newspaper articles and advertisements; and vandalism of Jewish cemeteries and attacks on funeral processions.

Parallel to these colonial incidents, the cultural and artistic world did not fare better in its treatment of Jews. The Elizabethan literary scene abounded with Jewish stereotypes in plays such as Christopher Marlowe's *The Jew of Malta*, as well as several others. Production of these plays in the colonies undoubtedly attracted large crowds and provided audiences with disagreeable depictions of Jews as scoundrels, monsters, and malicious villains.

The Spread of American Anti-Semitism

Despite negative imagery, random harassment, and attempts to exclude Jews and render them powerless, the population of American Jewry continued to grow. With the concentration of large Jewish populations in urban centers, there was a noticeable rise in American anti-Semitism that can be attributed mainly to economic and political factors.

The American system of free competition allowed Jews, among others, to gain influence in business, therefore challenging those who traditionally controlled large enterprises. Resentful, elite Americans began devising ways to isolate Jews. Their efforts were aimed at both restricting the Jewish people's ability to compete and blocking their entry into America's upper classes. Eventually, Jews were barred from some social clubs, residential districts, and hotels and resorts. The lower middle-classes, also envious, circulated claims that Jews were gaining positions of power through improper and questionable means.

8   THE DEARBORN INDEPENDENT

Jewish Power and America's Money Famine

The Warburg Federal Reserve Sucks Money to New York, Leaving Productive Sections of the Country in Disastrous Need

THE international Jewish banker who has no country but plays them all against one another, and the international Jewish proletariat that roams from land to land in search of a peculiar type of economic opportunity, are not figments of the imagination except to the non-Jew who prefers a lazy laxity of mind.

Of these classes of Jews, one or both are at the heart of the problems that disturb the world today. The immigration problem is Jewish. The money question is Jewish. The tie-up of world politics is Jewish. The terms of the Peace Treaty are Jewish. The diplomacy of the world is Jewish. The moral question in movies and theaters is Jewish. The mystery of the illicit liquor business is Jewish.

These facts are unfortunate as well as unpleasant for the Jew, and it is squarely up to him to deal with the facts, and not waste time in trying to destroy those who define the facts. These facts are interpreted by the Jew and the anti-Semite with strange extremes of blindness. The Jew never gets the world's point of view at all; he always gets the anti-Semite's point of view; and the anti-Semite is equally at fault in always getting the Jew's point of view. What both need is to get society's point of view, which is the one being set forth in this present series of articles.

Jews Must Try to Find Solution

VOLUME two of this series of Jewish Studies is now off the press. It is entitled "Jewish Activities in the United States," being the second volume of "The International Jew," twenty-two articles, 256 pages. Sent to any address at the cost of printing and mailing, which is 25 cents.

she speak? All that France sees is Otto H. Kahn! Why must a Jew represent the United States of America to France? When France supposedly speaks to the United States, through whom is it done? Through Viviani, Jewish in every thought and method. Now they are talking of sending Millerand over, another Jew. Britain sends Lord Reading. Germany sent Dr. Dernberg. And to other countries the United States sent Morgenthau, Strauss, Warburg, and lesser Jewlings.

It comes with something of a shock to learn that Foch is coming to the United States. We have not seen a Frenchman since Joffre visited us. It is good to see men of the white race come across the sea as if to reassure us that white men still live in those coun-

ized and stimulated among the people. That phase over, and money disappeared.

Is there any more tragic joke than that diligently disseminated in this country—"The United States has more gold than any other country in the world." Where is it? How long since you have seen a piece of gold? Where is all this gold—is it locked up in the Treasury of the United States Government? Why, that government is in debt, desperately trying to economize, cannot pay a soldier bonus because the finances of the country cannot stand it! Where is that gold? It may be *in* the United States, but it does not belong *to* the United States.

The American farmer, and those American industries which were not "wise" to the tricks of international Jewish bankers, and who were nipped by small loans, are wondering where all this money is. Furthermore, Europe, suffering from every possible lack, is looking to us and wondering where the money is.

Jewish Political and Financial Headquarters

THIS dispatch in a London paper may throw light on the matter: (italics are ours)

"It is learned that new gold shipments aggregating $2,800,000 are consigned to Kuhn, Loeb & Company, New York, making nearly $129,000,000 imported by that firm since the move-

Anti-Semitic propaganda from the 1920's, appearing in Henry Ford's newspaper the Dearborn Independent. (Library of Congress)

Meanwhile, on the European scene, a tide of anti-Semitism was sweeping Poland, Austria, and Russia, spawning similar feelings of hostility on the American continent. Following the infamous Russian pogroms of 1881-1882, thousands of immigrants took refuge in the United States. Although these refugees were easily absorbed at first, problems began developing later mainly over economic matters. Because the slow economy hit the middle-class the hardest, and because of the continuous competition from Jews, mostly with the middle-class, hostile feelings against Jews were greatly intensified.

The 1920's and the Ideologies of Hate

In the period beginning after World War I, especially in the 1920's, there was a significant increase in vehement and fanatic anti-Semitic movements and ideologies. One of the most virulent extremist movements of the 1920's was the Ku Klux Klan. Appealing to the less-educated and preaching propaganda against blacks, Jews, and Catholics, this movement sought to "purify" the United States of its racial pollution. The Klan also became an outlet for members of the Protestant American majority who harbored prejudice against other religious groups.

The 1920's also witnessed the circulation of the *Protocols of the Elders of Zion*, which was purported to be the master plan of a vast conspiracy of Jews aspiring to overthrow world governments and ultimately control the world. In reality, the *Protocols* were the work of Russian secret police agents and were widely distributed in the Soviet Union as well as in Arab countries. The publication of the *Protocols of the Elders of Zion* in the United States played a major role in inciting Jew-hatred and in promoting future anti-Semitic efforts. Henry Ford, the famed American automobile manufacturer, gave wide circulation to the *Protocols of the Elders of Zion* in his newspaper, the *Dearborn Independent*, where the forgery was reprinted.

> *Between 1920 and 1926, Henry Ford waged a vicious campaign of anti-Semitic propaganda in the* Dearborn Independent, *lashing out at a mythical conspiracy of international Jewry. With a mass circulation of 700,000, the* Dearborn Independent *also printed series of anti-Semitic articles and diatribes that incited the appearance of similar slanderous publications. The significance of Ford's tirades lies in the unprecedented push they gave for the entry of anti-Semitism in American politics, through the widespread support of his activities and his candidacy for president. Although Ford later formally apologized for promoting the forgery, he had already sown the seeds of overt anti-Semitism.*

The curtailment of Jewish immigration resulting from the laws of 1921 and 1924 and from the anti-immigrant stirrings of the postwar years diminished the frequency of overt anti-Semitism after 1927. In the Depression years of the 1930's, however, organized hatred of Jews reappeared with a new ferocity and on a scale greater than ever before.

Political Anti-semitism in the 1930's

During the 1930's, anti-Semitism drew its power not only from the Great Depression but also from the revolutionary and ideological right-wing extremism, the rise of Nazism in Germany, and the opposition to the Roosevelt New Deal, the economic and political policies that he adopted to advance economic recovery. With this decade, anti-Semitism made its first significant appearance on the political scene, and anti-Semitic organizations increased from nine in 1933 to 105 between 1934 and 1939.

Among the most important neo-fascist movements of the decade was the Union of Social Justice, organized by Father Charles E. Coughlin, a Catholic priest and an outspoken anti-Semite. Coughlin was a supporter of Adolf Hitler and, like Hitler, blamed the Depression on the Jews. Through his weekly radio programs, Coughlin's political propaganda reached millions of listeners. To draw his audience, Coughlin capitalized on the hardships and fright resulting from the Depression and on the tensions created by Communism. Support for his views, however, dropped sharply after the United States entered World War II against Germany.

Another anti-Semitic hatemonger of the 1930's and 1940's who became a national figure was Gerald L. K. Smith. Smith, a charismatic and brilliant orator, was at one time an associate of Coughlin, a Disciple of Christ minister, and a talented political organizer for Senator Huey P. Long of Louisiana. Smith pursued a political career, and, through association with Coughlin became a fervent anti-Semite. Subsequently, he founded the Committee of One Million, an organization aimed against Jews, Communists, and labor unions. The Committee of One Million was partly financed by Henry Ford, whose anti-Semitic views also influenced Smith. Smith became even more obssessed with hatred of Jews after his defeat for the U.S. Senate in 1942.

8   THE DEARBORN INDEPENDENT

Jewish Gamblers Corrupt American Baseball

"The Cleanest Sport" Near Its Doom From "Too Much Jew." Baseball Has Passed Under Control of "the Sport Spoilers." Can It Be Saved?

THERE are men in the United States who say that baseball has received its death wound and is slowly dying out of the list of respectable sports. There are other men who say that American baseball can be saved if a clean sweep is made of the Jewish influence which has just dragged it through a period of bitter shame and demoralization.

Whether baseball as a first-class sport is killed and will survive only as a cheap-jack entertainment; or whether baseball possesses sufficient intrinsic character to rise in righteous wrath and cast out the danger that menaces it, will remain a matter of various opinion. But there is one certainty, namely, that the last and most dangerous blow dealt baseball was curiously notable for its Jewish character.

Yet only lesser Jews were indicted. Inevitably the names of other Jews appeared in the press accounts, and people wondered who they were. A Jewish judge presided. Jewish lawyers were prominent on both sides of the cases. Numerous strange things occurred.

But strangest of all is the fact that although American fans felt that something epochal had happened in baseball, few really know what it is.

There has been time enough for others to tell the truth if they were so disposed. Many sport editors have come as near telling it as their newspapers would permit them. But it becomes daily more evident that if the whole matter is to be laid bare, so that Americans may know where to look for danger, THE DEARBORN INDEPENDENT will have to do it.

Jews Are Not Good Sportsmen

AND this is not of our own choosing. Baseball is a trivial matter compared with some of the facts that

VOLUME two of this series of Jewish Studies is now off the press. It is entitled "Jewish Activities in the United States," being the second volume of "The International Jew," twenty-two articles, 256 pages. Sent to any address at the cost of printing and mailing, which is 25 cents.

and nearly destroying our cleanest, most manly public sports.

It is worth noting that in Chicago, where the Jewish Anti-Defamation League has its headquarters, there was not a word of reproof sent out from Jews to the Jewish culprits, chiding them for their activities. Not a word. But at the same time the pressure of the Anti-Defamation League was heavy on the whole American newspaper press to prevent the public statement that the whole baseball scandal was a Jewish performance from end to end.

Baseball had a close call for its life back in 1875. Rowdyism, gambling, drinking and general disorderliness on the baseball fields brought the sport very low in public estimation, so low that attendance at the games fell heavily.

In this year 1921 there is another public rebuke being administered baseball by the same means—a very heavy reduction of public support in attendance at the games.

The storm began to be heard as far back as 1919.

the first one. Two of these men were Carl Zork and Benny Franklin who were just as much implicated at the time of the first grand jury as at the second, but the prosecutor's office did not try to secure their indictment. Why? Because Replogle, the attorney representing the prosecution, said there were enough men indicted without Zork and Franklin. These two St. Louis Jews were represented by Alfred S. Austrian, a Jewish lawyer, of Chicago.

This second grand jury also indicted Ben and Louis Levi and their brother-in-law, D. A. Zelser, gamblers from Des Moines. Their indictment was not secured at the first grand jury investigation directed by Replogle, assistant to Hoyne who was then acting for the state of Illinois. Between the first and second grand juries a political change had occurred, and the public interests in the second grand jury were in the care of a new prosecuting attorney, Robert Crowe, a former judge.

"Who's Who" of Jews in Baseball

IT BECOMES necessary at this point in the narrative to give a brief "Who's Who" of the baseball scandal, omitting from the list the names of the baseball players who are sufficiently known to the public. This list will comprise only those who have been in the background of baseball and whom it is necessary to know in order to understand what has been happening behind the scenes in recent years.

For the first name let us take Albert D. Lasker. He is a member of the American Jewish Committee, was recently appointed by President Harding to be chairman of the United States Shipping Board, and is known as the author of the "Lasker Plan," a widely heralded plan for the reorganization of baseball, which practically

More anti-Semitic propaganda from the Dearborn Independent, *blaming "Jewish gamblers" for the 1919 Black Sox scandal and hinting at a larger Jewish conspiracy.* (Library of Congress)

American Universities and Discrimination

Beginning in the 1870's and continuing until the 1970's, barriers were erected restricting the entrance of Jews to colleges, universities, and professional schools, including medical, dental, and law schools. Jewish quotas were set as early as the 1870's and increased with the influx of Jewish immigrants and the varying patterns of anti-Semitism. Between 1918 and 1947, the number of schools in the East imposing Jewish quotas increased, with more schools in other parts of the nations following suit. It was only after 1948, with the growth of civil rights and anti-discrimination movements, that the quotas began declining.

Institutions that placed enrollment restrictions against Jews played a major role in the economy by seeking to strengthen the position of native-born white Anglo-Saxon Protestants and by weakening the academic advancement and eventual professional influence of the Jewish people. College administrators, influenced by racist ideas, believed that students of Anglo-Saxon and Nordic descents were more intelligent and therefore more desirable. School officials also believed that by imposing quotas they were helping to prevent anti-Semitism from increasing. Others were concerned with preserving the homogeneity of students on campuses and worried about the educational mobility of Jews and the possibility that they might overcrowd universities.

The democratic nature of the American government provides for the equal treatment of all its citizens. Because of such essential beliefs and protections, the government has never sanctioned anti-Semitism, and hence discrimination against Jews has been more difficult to detect. Anti-Semitic hate sheets and movements attracted a small portion of the American population, but it was the less visible, or more "civil," discriminatory measures that occurred more widely and that hurt the Jews the most.

5 The Jewish American Community

The Jewish American community, from its beginnings, was established by Jews who did not need to struggle for their civil rights and had no inclination to lead a traditional Jewish life. Many of those who came to the New World from 1654 until the 1920's were the most cosmopolitan of poor European Jewry. These immigrants came to America to do business, not to devote themselves to their religion. Their talent for commerce, combined with a need for entrepreneurial middlemen in the American economy, allowed them quick upward mobility.

As if their long history in exile prepared them to flourish in America, the Jews soon achieved disproportionate influence for their small numbers. The successful American Jews were able to organize a Jewish community based on religious association, which also allowed them to preserve their heritage and simultaneously function in a secular society like everyone else.

The Place of Religion in American Society

Judaism, along with Protestantism and Catholicism, became one of America's three major religions, placing both benefits and responsibilities on Jews. The demands of American life added further opportunities for Jews to participate in the making of a new nation. Nevertheless, American Jewry was lowest in the hierarchy and has had the least influence of the three religious groups. To safeguard their position as fully legitimate Americans, "defense" organizations were created to break barriers that Jews considered anti-Semitic. Thus, American Jews have organized themselves fully within the framework of American society to handle the business of their survival and the preservation of the American way.

The individualistic nature of American society greatly influenced the character of the American Jewish community. Individual Jews were free to participate or not to participate in Jewish affairs. The separation of church and state in American culture slotted religion in the private domain. For many Jews, keeping to one's faith became a personal matter to be exercised in one's leisure time at best. At the same time, in this relaxed religious environment, the rate of intermarriage continually

Traditional elements of Jewish life are displayed at this wedding reception—silver kiddush cups holding the sacramental wine; the braided challah bread; and the yarmulkes covering the men's heads. (Debra Picker)

increased and more and more Jews led secular lives, threatening the survival of the American Jewish community from within.

Divisions within Judaism appeared, offering different interpretations of the ancient faith. Jewish denominations sprang up competing for worshippers, imitating Protestant denominations and their congregation-based practices. In fact, the organizational patterns of American Jewry were very similar to those of Protestants. The main reason for this has been the Judeo-Christian worldview that Protestants and Jews have shared to a great extent in the United States. Jews simply fit in or easily adjusted to a generally hospitable environment in America, achieving enough comfort and security to redirect the old religion to the realities of the New World.

Reform Judaism

The Reform movement, which sprang up in Charleston, South Carolina, in 1824, and then gained momentum in the Midwest during the 1850's, was the first to reform its services. Conducted mostly in English and not only in the ancient Hebrew, Reform services resembled Protestant services in structure. The changes included the introduction of a new prayerbook and eliminating prayers that were thought to be no longer compatible with modern realities. An organ, a mixed choir, and family pews were also introduced, eliminating the separation of men and women, and worship with bared heads was allowed. Late Friday evening services were created for Jews unable to reach the synagogue in time for the traditionally required sunset Sabbath worship. Prohibitions regarding the observance of the Sabbath were loosened, since Jews worked on Saturday like other Americans. Equality was given to women in synagogue rituals, conversion was made easier due to increasing mixed marriages, and dietary laws were eased to fit patterns distinctive to the United States and the Americanization of its Jews.

Under the leadership of Isaac Mayer Wise, the Reform movement attempted to unite all American Jewry under its

Women are rabbis in many Reform Jewish congregations. (Bill Aron/PhotoEdit)

banner, but disputes with more traditional Jews over the reforms made this an impossible goal. In addition, the Reform movement found it difficult to attract new immigrants who had not yet undergone the process of Americanization. By 1937, the Reform movement began to return to some of the traditional practices in Judaism. Skullcaps and prayer shawls are now worn as an option in Reform temples, and a new prayerbook includes more traditional liturgy.

Conservative Judaism

The second major movement to emerge within American Judaisms was the Conservative movement, which was created by more traditional Jews in response to competition from Reform. Centered in Philadelphia, the Conservative movement blended traditionalism with flexibility in dealing with the modern world. Conservative Jews preferred a more traditional brand of Judaism while being fully American. Isaac Leeser, a Philadelphian who was the most dynamic leader of nineteenth century American Jewry was spokesman for the Conservative movement. He also translated the Jewish Bible into English, created the first major Jewish newspaper in the United States, and inspired the founding of a Jewish Seminary in New York.

Because it made a place for traditional Jewish beliefs and practices without demanding a marked separation from the larger society, Conservatism became the largest Jewish religious movement in the United States. Conservative Judaism was particularly appealing to the large numbers of Jews who had emigrated from Eastern Europe and who wanted to preserve the more traditional form of worship they were accustomed to. These Jews were unwilling to abandon the head covering, the dietary practices observed on a daily basis, and some of the traditional readings from the Torah on major Jewish holidays.

Jewish Orthodoxy

The third major religious movement to emerge in organized form was Jewish American Orthodoxy. From its beginnings centered in New York, Orthodoxy was established by Eastern European immigrants who, even more than their Conservative counterparts, were deeply committed to traditional Judaism as practiced in Europe and passed on by their fathers. Orthodoxy rejected all changes in the observance of the Sabbath, liturgy, and family religious practices, and it demanded strict adherence to all Jewish religious laws. Orthodox Jews preferred their rabbis to dress in the traditional black garments, and they wanted their children to receive a traditional Jewish religious education, studying the Torah and the writings of the great rabbis throughout the centuries.

Orthodoxy was unable to attract new worshippers because of its traditional attitudes toward women, not allowing them full equality in the synagogue. American Orthodoxy was infused, however, by immigrants escaping the Nazis and the Holocaust in

Hasids conducting naming ceremony after the bris (or circumcision) for a Jewish baby boy.
(Bill Aron/PhotoEdit)

Europe. These new immigrants did not come to the United States in search of a better life but because their very lives were in danger. They also came with a notion that Jewish life in the United States was not quite Jewish. Among the refugees were Hasidic groups who believed themselves to be the upholders of true Judaism. The strongest of the Hasidic groups is Chabad; though small in number, Chabad may be the most dynamic Jewish religious movement today. Chabad is active in almost every major city in the United States, working to attract American Jews to traditional orthodox Judaism.

Reconstructionism

By far the smallest and most obscure religious movement in American Judaism is Reconstructionism. Founded in 1920 by Mordecai M. Kaplan, a Conservative Jew, Reconstructionism was inspired by sociological, philosophical, religious, and educational ideas of the modern era. Kaplan believed that Judaism is a "religious civilization" encompassing nationhood, language, folk custom, art, and the like, and are all essential to its preservation. Reconstructionism has not attracted many Jews because most Reform and Conservative Jews are unable to accept its free approach radically diluting Jewish practices and beliefs. Reconstructionist ideas, though, have penetrated the consciousness of American Jewry.

Adjustments in Role, Form, and Content

The impact of the United States on Jewish religious life can also be seen in the radical change of the role of the rabbi. In Europe, the rabbi was usually deeply orthodox and steeped in Jewish learning, whereas in the United States, the rabbi serves his congregation as a professional leader of the synagogue, much like a Protestant minister. Mixed seating of men and women during services was introduced in American synagogues and today is taken for granted in all Reform and nearly all Conservative congregations as well as some Orthodox synagogues. The form and content of services have also been strongly influenced by American life. The Jewish rhythm of daily services has shifted to weekly services on the Sabbath. Indeed, the content of the service has shifted from emphasis on Torah reading to the sermon. Nevertheless, American Jews feel entitled to have their great holidays included on the American calendar, in equal standing with the great Christian holidays.

Jewish holidays begin with Rosh Hashanah (in September), considered "New Year Day," which celebrates the creation of the universe and hence the beginning of all things. Ten days later, Yom Kippur (September-October) is observed for twenty-four hours of prayer and fasting, designed to achieve spiritual regeneration through atonement. Hanukkah, which usually falls close to Christmas, refers to the kindling of lights symbolizing the hope of the Jewish people, while Passover, which falls around the time of Easter, commemorates the Israelite escape from slavery in Egypt under the leadership of Moses at about 1200 B.C.

National Organizations Maintain Jewish Identity

The American Jewish community of some six million people can be perceived as a nonterritorial "state" within a state. Designed to maintain Jewish identity, the Jewish community is much like its American model. There is no single governing body but several decision-making organizations with specialized fields of interest. The closest to being a nationwide umbrella organization is the Council of Jewish Federations and Welfare Funds (CJF), whose annual General Assembly has become the most important meeting of the American Jewish community.

The federations are the most government-like institutions within American Jewry, providing comprehensive services to Jewish communities. Since the first federation was founded in

The Sedar table at Passover; a Jewish family learns the meaning of Passover, as explained by the grandfather. (Gregory Teitelbaum)

Boston in 1895, the role of the federations has evolved from mainly being concerned with helping new immigrants and the needy to encompassing all aspects of Jewish life and concerns. Some eight hundred communities, organized through about three hundred federations, raise funds that are disbursed to provide needed services in the Jewish community, on a countrywide, regional, and local basis.

Other general-purpose organizations express the various concerns in the American Jewish community. The American Jewish Committee and the American Jewish Congress are elite organizations whose members are strategically placed among the leadership in major institutions and synagogues. Zionist organizations in the United States have again gained momentum since the Six Day War of 1967, articulating support for Israel. Officially known as the Women's Zionist Organization, Hadassah is most likely the largest Jewish organization in the United States. Though anti-Semitism in the United States was really severe only between 1870 and World War II, nevertheless the Anti-Defamation League keeps a watchful eye for any discriminatory acts against Jewish Americans.

Jewish Overseas Organizations

   Jewish American organizations that deal with Jewish issues overseas are the best organized and the best integrated of all organizations within the Jewish American community. As the descendants of immigrants who escaped from the countries that persecuted and murdered them, Americans have always felt a deep concern for their coreligionists in peril abroad. The American Jewish Joint Distribution Committee is well known for its efforts to help European Jewry after the devastation of World War I and the impoverishment caused by the rise of Anti-Semitism and the Nazi era. During World War II, the JOINT, as

A menorah; the Jewish American community has experienced a resurgence of interest in traditional Judaism. (Bill Aron/PhotoEdit)

it is known, clandestinely delivered hard currency to the desperate Warsaw ghetto. With the money, the remaining besieged Jews were able to buy a few arms they used in a heroic uprising against the Germans.

After the tragedy of the Holocaust, the reestablishment of a Jewish homeland in Israel inspired the Jewish American community to support the small nation in its desperate struggle against the Arabs. Organizations such as the United Jewish Appeal and others raised vast sums of money for the fledgling state. On the political front, Jewish organizations used their influence in Washington, D.C. to drum up support for Israel. The most powerful pro-Israeli Jewish American organizations to emerge is the American Israel Public Affairs Committee, known as AIPAC. Sometimes referred to as the Jewish lobby, AIPAC achieved its power by being able to organize important constituencies of Jews across the United States to vote in local elections for candidates supportive of aid to Israel and other Jewish concerns. Though AIPAC has come under scrutiny in recent years, the organization operates no differently than any other American special-interest lobby.

Today, the Jewish community in the United States is better organized than ever. The flight to the suburbs, which at first caused organizational problems, has now been mainly overcome. The vast Los Angeles area, for example, has become one of the best organized Jewish communities in the United States. American Jews reside today in more towns and small cities in the United States than at anytime in the past.

Because Jews now live in a United States relatively free of anti-Semitism, the rate of intermarriage and assimilation has increased dramatically. Studies have found that fifty-two percent of Jews marry non-Jews and seventy percent of their children are raised either in Christianity or with no religion at all. Some Jewish leaders have warned that the very survival of Judaism in the United States will be threatened if these trends continue. Furthermore, less than half of the 6.0 million American Jews consider themselves part of a religious group. Support for Israel

and the memory of the Holocaust have been the focus of Jewish
identity in recent times, not a search for the Jewish understanding
of faith and God.

As a result, Jewish organizations are shifting their attention to
promoting Judaism in the United States as well as carrying the
burden of Jewish interests overseas and fighting anti-Semitism.
The federations, which traditionally stayed away from religious
involvement, are now attempting to work closer with synagogues
and Jewish cultural and educational institutions to preserve
Jewish identity. Meanwhile, there are encouraging signs that there
is a new interest in religion emerging in the Jewish American
community. Enrollment at rabbinical schools in all the major
branches of Judaism has increased, and new synagogues have
sprouted throughout the country.

Jewish Population in the United States, 1990

State	Estimated Jewish Population	Total Population*
Alabama	9,300	4,102,000
Alaska	2,400	524,000
Arizona	71,500	3,489,000
Arkansas	2,000	2,345,000
California	919,500	28,314,000
Colorado	50,000	3,301,000
Connecticut	113,200	3,233,000
Delaware	9,500	660,000
District of Columbia	25,400	617,000
Florida	567,000	12,335,000
Georgia	72,500	6,342,000
Hawaii	7,000	1,098,000
Idaho	450	1,003,000
Illinois	257,400	11,614,000
Indiana	18,300	5,556,000
Iowa	6,350	2,834,000
Kansas	14,000	2,495,000
Kentucky	11,800	3,727,000
Louisiana	15,700	4,408,000
Maine	8,400	1,205,000

Jewish Population in the United States, 1990 (continued)

State	Estimated Jewish Population	Total Population*
Maryland	211,000	4,622,000
Massachusetts	276,000	5,889,000
Michigan	107,300	9,240,000
Minnesota	30,500	4,307,000
Mississippi	1,900	2,620,000
Missouri	61,600	5,141,000
Montana	450	805,000
Nebraska	7,400	1,602,000
Nevada	20,500	1,054,000
New Hampshire	7,000	1,085,000
New Jersey	430,000	7,721,000
New Mexico	6,400	1,507,000
New York	1,843,000	17,909,000
North Carolina	16,300	6,489,000
North Dakota	750	667,000
Ohio	130,800	10,855,000
Oklahoma	5,300	3,242,000
Oregon	12,500	2,767,000
Pennsylvania	330,500	12,001,000
Rhode Island	16,100	993,000
South Carolina	9,300	3,470,000
South Dakota	350	713,000
Tennessee	19,400	4,895,000
Texas	109,000	16,841,000
Utah	3,100	1,690,000
Vermont	4,800	557,000
Virginia	67,600	6,015,000
Washington	32,800	4,648,000
West Virgina	2,400	1,876,000
Wisconsin	34,700	4,855,000
Wyoming	450	479,000
U.S. TOTAL	**5,981,000	245,807,000

N.B. Details may not add to totals because of rounding.

*Resident population, July 1, 1988. (*Source:* U.S. Bureau of the Census, *Current Population Reports,* series P-25, no. 1044.)

**Exclusive of Puerto Rico and the Virgin Islands which previously reported Jewish populations of 1,500 and 350, respectively.

6 America and the Holocaust

When American and other Allied troops finally defeated Germany in 1945, what they found in Nazi-occupied Europe was the most horrific killing machine in the history of humankind. Concentration camps filled with thousands of people on the verge of starvation brought Allied troops to tears. Slave labor camps numbering in the thousands were discovered throughout Germany, and mass graves were found everywhere. Most shocking, however, were the extermination camps found by the Russian armies in Poland, where millions of people were gassed to death and then their corpses were burned, leaving little trace of their existence. The overwhelming majority of the victims were Europe's Jews, who were singled out by the Nazis for extinction.

A Troubling Reality

The full impact of the atrocities and the staggering death toll of Jews reached the American public in the form of newsreels shown in motion picture theaters throughout the United States. Explicit films of the most inhumane "living conditions," torture chambers, and methods of mass murder sent shock waves through the Jewish-American community and the United States at large. Heartbreaking scenes of mounds of shoes, clothing, children's toys, and eyeglasses taken from the victims, and piles of gold fillings extracted from the teeth of corpses revolted Americans and the world.

While Americans were basking in the glory of victory over Germany and Japan, an undercurrent of guilt and responsibility over what was allowed to be done to the Jews troubled the American conscience. Returning American troops, who told their families and friends of the indescribable horrors that they witnessed in Germany and elsewhere, brought the Holocaust home to the average American household. American anti-Semitism and the relative silence of the revered Franklin Delano Roosevelt throughout World War II proved to be troubling realities to the American sense of justice. Jewish Americans, who had almost unanimously voted for Roosevelt in four presidential elections, felt betrayed by the great leader, who did not live to see the end of the war and the evidence of Nazi crimes.

The Press and the Holocaust

During the war, the American press provided limited coverage of the extent of the tragedy unfolding in Europe. Rarely did major American newspapers print stories about the mass murder of European Jews on the front page. Minimizing the importance of these events, articles were usually placed on the back pages of newspapers, and the wording gave readers the impression that the extent of the atrocities was unsubstantiated. Though the mass murder of Jews was done in secrecy and under wartime conditions, there were reliable witnesses. Polish couriers on missions to England and a few prominent anti-Nazi Germans provided detailed information about the systematic elimination of European Jewry.

The skeptical reporting of Nazi crimes in the American press can be attributed to a number of divergent and yet overlapping factors originating before World War II. One of the most compelling and yet least known explanations is the fact that many distinguished Americans, including leading journalists, finished

Jewish victims from the Gusen Concentration camp, near Linz, Austria. (National Archives)

their education in German universities, as was fashionable during the period between the two wars. They could not fathom the disturbing reports about a country and a people they considered among the most civilized in the world. In 1936, well after severe persecution of Jews was legalized in Germany, Adolf Hitler made the cover of *Time* magazine as "Man of the Year"; the cover story noted his success in rebuilding Germany.

The Jewish press in the United States reported the Holocaust much more accurately. The most detailed accounts could be found in the Yiddish language newspapers, which generally did not go beyond the readership of the Yiddish speaking Jewish-American community. Even the Yiddish press, however, could not comprehend the full extent of the despicable horror inflicted upon Europe's Jews by the Germans and their friends.

The United States Enters the War

When the United States finally entered World War II, it was not against the well-known evils of Nazism but in response to a sneak attack on Pearl Harbor on December 7, 1941, by Germany's ally, Japan. At the time, few knew that on December 8, 1941, Chelmno, the first death camp, located near the Polish city of Lodz, had become operational. Unlike Auschwitz, with its sophisticated gas chambers and efficient crematoria, Chelmno was a crude operation. Jewish men, women, and children who had been starved by the Germans since the winter of 1939 were transported to Chelmno in groups of nine hundred per day. Easily controlled in such small numbers, they were then forced into airtight trucks, some eighty persons per truck. Once the doors were locked, hoses from the engine delivered carbon monoxide to the interior, slowly asphyxiating the Jews inside. The ride lasted between fifteen and twenty minutes to a nearby forest, where the corpses were dumped into mass graves. Those who were not yet dead were shot in the head. Approximately 360,000 Jews were murdered in Chelmno alone, before it was dismantled in June, 1944.

Stephen Samuel Wise, a leader in the Jewish American community who helped sway public opinion against Hitler before the U.S. entered World War II. (Library of Congress)

Could Europe's Jews have been rescued? Why didn't the
United States absorb large numbers of Jewish refugees before the
war, when severe persecution of Jews began? Why did the United
States turn back shiploads of desperate Jews during the war,
when it was well known by government officials what would
happen to them once they were returned to Europe? Did the
United States do all it could to prevent the mass murders? Did
the Jewish-American community do enough for its brothers and
sisters in Europe? Why weren't the death camps in Poland
bombed by the Allies? Was Roosevelt an anti-Semite who
pretended to be a friend of the Jews? These questions and more
have haunted Jews everywhere since the revelations at the end of
the war.

Roosevelt, Congress, and American Jewry

The Jews, who throughout their history depended on
benevolent leaders for their survival, in the 1930's gave their
passionate support to Roosevelt. Threatened by infectious anti-
Semitism spreading in Europe and to the United States, Jewish
Americans felt comfortable with Roosevelt, who brought more
Jews into the upper levels of government than ever before in
American history. Roosevelt, however, played the role of
"protector" for everyone, not only for Jews. He liked to be
addressed as "Papa" or "Chief." At the time, it was unimaginable
to Jews that such a president would fail to protect their brothers
and sisters in Europe if their situation became desperate.

Since the war, American Jews have been accused of not doing
enough to help the Jews of Europe. Some have suggested that
American Jewry feared for its own survival in the United States
in the face of what seemed at the time an unstoppable anti-
Semitic tide. However, the attempts by the Jewish-American
community to loosen immigration restrictions, which would have
allowed more European Jews to escape, backfired. Reflecting the
attitudes of the time, the Congress of the United States did not

respond to Jewish pressure. Jews felt that the only course of action was to appeal to Roosevelt and other American leaders in private.

While members of the German-American Bund, America's Nazi party, fought with American Jews in the streets, some prominent Americans advanced the cause of Nazism. Charles Lindbergh, the famous aviator and a national hero, publicly defended Hitler and worked diligently to prevent the United States' entry into the war against Germany. After the Nazis implemented the anti-Jewish Nuremberg Laws of 1935, the United States debated whether or not to participate in the 1936 Berlin Olympics in protest. Avery Brundage, the chairman of the United States Olympic Committe, also publicly defended Nazi Germany and succeeded in ensuring the United States' participation in the games.

Anti-Immigration Laws

In the domestic political arena, widely accepted opposition to loosening immigration laws, established in 1924, prevented the rescue of large numbers of European Jews. The "restrictionists" argued that refugees who came to the United States would take away jobs belonging to American workers hard hit by high unemployment caused by the Great Depression. The anti-immigration forces wielded substantial political power in Congress, which was reinforced by strong currents of nativism or "100 percent Americanism" and was often linked to anti-Semitism. Even during the war, hundreds of bills were introduced in Congress to limit immigration. The plain truth was that Americans were prejudiced against Jews, which contributed greatly to Roosevelt's reaction to the Holocaust.

The first time Roosevelt tried to intervene on behalf of European Jewry was in 1938, when Austria merged with Germany and its Jews were severely mistreated. Roosevelt floated the possibility of helping Austrian Jews but was advised that

Congress would not extend the immigration quota. Roosevelt then called for an international conference of some thirty-two nations, held in France, but few agreed to accept any new immigrants. Later the same year, when the Nazis orchestrated a nationwide pogrom against Jews in Germany, called Crystal Night, Roosevelt extended visitors' visas, which ultimately allowed nearly fifteen thousand German Jews to remain in the United States permanently. By then, however, Roosevelt was convinced that America would have to fight against Hitler in Europe. Because of American anti-Semitism, Roosevelt did not want to be seen to be too involved in the question of Jews. Roosevelt was now becoming more sympathetic to the plight of Jews but for political reasons was only willing to express that sympathy through quiet administrative action. Nevertheless, because of Roosevelt's efforts, 110,000 Jews were admitted to the United States between 1938 and 1941, when the United States entered the war.

Anti-Semitism was particularly virulent in Poland; ironically, many Poles themselves became victims of Nazi Germany's doctrine of racial superiority. (Lee Peterson/Photobank)

Germany's Jews and Nazi European Expansions

Hitler's irrational and fanatical hatred of Jews infected almost every country in Europe, as well as the United States and Canada. In Germany, prior to World War II, there were only about half a million Jews in the midst of eighty million Germans. Most of the German Jews were assimilated, and many of them strongly identified with German culture, to which they had made notable contributions. Hitler blamed all Germany's ills on this relatively tiny number of Jews, who clearly lacked the power attributed to them by anti-Semites. Nevertheless, Hitler's racist propaganda machine cunningly drew on fears and suspicions nourished by centuries of Christian and European anti-Semitism—reviving a tradition of hatred that seemed to have been on the decline.

When Germany invaded Poland on September 1, 1939, triggering World War II, the Nazis suddenly trapped nearly three million Polish Jews. Soon afterward France, Belgium, and Holland fell. Now the Nazis also had Western European Jews, including some of those who managed to escape from Germany. On June 22, 1941, Hitler's forces invaded the Soviet Union and the Baltic States, leaving another several million Jews under Nazi control. Already living in ghettos and subject to virulent anti-Semitism, Polish Jews were the easiest for the Germans to identify and isolate, with the help of the local populations. The Nazis simply closed off Jewish neighborhoods or herded Jews into the oldest and most decrepit sections of Polish cities, surrounding them with barbed wire fences, walls, and armed guards.

The first mass killings of Jews occurred simultaneously with the invasion of the Soviet Union. Special killing units followed closely behind regular German armies as they pushed deeper and deeper into the Soviet Union. Some of the members of these units had been in German prisons for horrible acts of murder. Under the cover of war the Nazis used local anti-Semites in the

Numbers of Jews Murdered in Nazi Death Camps in Poland:

Auschwitz/Birkenau 2,100,000
Belzec 600,000
Chelmno 360,000
Majdanek 360,000
Sorbibor 250,000
Treblinka 830,000

Ukraine, Byelorussia, Lithuania, Latvia, and Estonia to lead
these units to Jewish villages. One million Jews were rounded up,
forced to strip naked, and then shot by firing squads in places
such as Babi Yar, near the city of Kiev in the Ukraine.

The first death camps with their various types of gas were
introduced because killing by firing squads was too slow and not
"elegant" in the judgment of the German high command. Some
of the shooters, hardened, Jew-hating murderers who took coffee
and lunch breaks near the mass graves, nevertheless suffered
nervous breakdowns. Realizing the enormity of their crime, the
Nazis also wanted to leave as little evidence as possible. At a
death camp called Treblinka, for example, Jewish slaves were
forced to unearth hundreds of thousands of partially decomposed
corpses, which were then burned in heaps. The problem of
bodies was solved by the Germans when crematoria were added
to the camps, where Jews were cremated soon after gassing,
leaving only ash.

American Caution and Rescue Efforts

At first, uncertainty over the outcome of the war prevented
Roosevelt and others from publicly speaking out against the
atrocities. German military victories stunned the world. For a
time it appeared that the Nazis were unstoppable and even
America might fall under Nazi terror and Japanese aggression in

the Pacific. Being on the side of the Jews was not good politics. Wherever Germany reigned, those who helped Jews were either severely punished or killed. In 1943, however, as the war turned against both Germany and Japan and Allied victory seemed inevitable, the possibility of rescuing the remainder of European Jewry became a hotly contested argument within Roosevelt's cabinet.

The main opposition to the rescue came from the State Department and the Foreign Office, where some influential figures argued that a large-scale operation to rescue Jews would detract from the war effort, delay victory, and cost American lives. Finally, after fourteen months of bickering, when President Roosevelt saw that a rescue resolution was going to pass in the Senate, he went ahead and immediately issued an executive order establishing the War Refugee Board on January 22, 1944.

The War Refugee Board (WRB) resulted from persistent appeals for action by the Treasury Department, under Morgenthau, and various Jewish organizations. However, soon after its establishment, Jewish leaders were disheartened to find out that the WRB could not get government funds to conduct its rescue operation. Once again, the burden fell on the Jewish-American community, which contributed nearly $20 million, while Roosevelt allotted a little more than $1.5 million from the President's Emergency Fund. Escape hatches were found in Turkey, Spain, Southern Italy, Sweden, and Switzerland, where small numbers of Jews were saved. Some Jews were also rescued from Croatian Nazis in Yugoslavia, but large-scale rescue operations never materialized. The State and War departments, directed to help the WRB, often stood in the way of rescue. The Pentagon refused to consider bombing Auschwitz from bases in Northern Italy, sticking to its policy to end the war as quickly as possible, while 480,000 Hungarian Jews were turned into ashes.

In the final analysis, six million Jews were brutally murdered because, with the exception of a small number of individual human beings, no nation, including the United States, cared enough to help them.

Estimated Number of Jews Killed
in the Final Solution

Country	Estimated Pre-Final Solution Population	Estimated Jewish Population Annihilated	
		Number	Percent
Poland	3,300,000	3,000,000	90
Baltic countries	253,000	228,000	90
Germany/Austria	240,000	210,000	90
Protectorate	90,000	80,000	89
Slovakia	90,000	75,000	83
Greece	70,000	54,000	77
The Netherlands	140,000	105,000	75
Hungary	650,000	450,000	70
SSR White Russia	375,000	245,000	65
SSR Ukraine*	1,500,000	900,000	60
Belgium	65,000	40,000	60
Yugoslavia	43,000	26,000	60
Rumania	600,000	300,000	50
Norway	1,800	900	50
France	350,000	90,000	26
Bulgaria	64,000	14,000	22
Italy	40,000	8,000	20
Luxembourg	5,000	1,000	20
Russia (RSFSR)*	975,000	107,000	11
Denmark	8,000	—	—
Finland	2,000	—	—
Total	8,861,800	5,933,900	67

*The Germans did not occupy all the territory of this republic.

7 Zionism

The term "Zionism," which derives from the name of a citadel in ancient Jerusalem, has been used in two quite different ways. Introduced in the 1890's, the term referred to the worldwide Jewish movement aimed at the creation of a Jewish state in Palestine. People who belonged to this movement proudly referred to themselves as Zionists.

Since 1948, however, when the State of Israel emerged, the term "Zionism" has been used in another way, referring to support for Israel and its development, and in particular referring to support for Israel's defense. People who are critical of Israel and its supporters in the United States often use the word "Zionist" as an accusation. Both senses of the word are rooted in the historical claims of the Jewish people to the land of Palestine.

Fundamental Controversies and Ancient Longings

Any discussion of the attachment of Jews to the ancient region of Palestine must acknowledge the fundamental and persistent controversy between Jews and Arabs, based on differing interpretations of history. Zionists believe that Jews have a right to establish a state in Palestine because it was the "land of their fathers" almost two thousand years ago. Palestinians, however, although they recognize the existence of ancient Hebrew kingdoms in Palestine, believe that the Hebrews were one transitory conqueror among many, and that ancient conquests do not justify the creation of a state in the twentieth century. Zionists also refer to the Bible to support the Jewish claim to Palestine, citing God's promise to give the land of Palestine to the Hebrews and their descendants: the "Promised Land" to the "Chosen People." To Palestinians, religion has no place in secular world politics; however, in the view of all Arabs, including the Palestinians, the Jewish state is seen as an intruder in the Muslim world.

Regardless of the numerous controversies, it remains true that the longing to return to Israel has always been a traditional and spiritual cause for the Jewish people, long before Zionism became an organized political movement. Most early efforts to revive Jewish nationalism, however, only kept the dream alive; they had limited impact on world Jewry and did not inspire a mass movement to Palestine. It was not until the arrival of Theodor Herzl on the European scene and the first world Zionist congress in 1897 that Zionism became a political force.

Theodor Herzl

Herzl's publication of *Der Judenstaat* (*The Jewish State: An Attempt at a Modern Solution of the Jewish Question*) in 1896 launched Zionism into a modern political movement. Herzl, a well-known Viennese journalist, basically stated the following in his book: Jewish assimilation has failed; anti-Semitism is increasing at a rapid pace; the Jews are one people; and they are entitled to a state.

This was nothing new. What was revolutionary and daring about Herzl's proposal was that he intended to create the Jewish state *with* the assistance of the great European powers. In the early stages of the movement, many Jews in Europe and the United States felt that Zionism constituted a threat to their assimilation and feared that it might bring a resurgence of anti-Semitism. Despite waves of protest, Herzl, at the first world Zionist congress, still reached one of his aims: He gathered world Jewish leaders to examine collectively the future of their people, and he established a public and official forum to confer on Zionism. After the congress ended, Herzl noted in his diary: "At Basle I founded the Jewish state. If I said this out loudly today, I would be greeted by universal laughter. In five years, perhaps, and certainly in fifty years, everyone will perceive it." Herzl died seven years after the first congress, but he was not too far off in his prediction: Israel came into existence on May 15, 1948, less than fifty-one years after that diary entry.

Nationalism and the Rise of Zionism

What motivated Herzl and others to pursue the founding of a Jewish state? Zionism was born in an age of European nationalism and colonialism. After the freedoms brought by the Enlightenment and the French Revolution in the eighteenth century, the hopes of Jews were shattered by the rise of European nationalism. This powerful political movement advocated devotion to one's state and appealed to a common past, a past from which Jews were excluded. Therefore, while the Enlightenment encouraged the equal treatment of Jews, nationalism at the same time said that Jews could never be accepted as equal European citizens.

Despite this setback, Western Jews were assimilating and taking up their new obligations and loyalties as equal citizens of their respective states. This new freedom, however, was accompanied by a traumatic loss of self-identity. Influenced by the spirit of nationalism but at the same time enduring its repercussions, Jews began to examine their new situation as emancipated European citizens. Would they have to give up their culture, religion, and traditions? Would they have to fight Jews from other European states? Was total assimilation possible? Did their people constitute a separate national group entitled to its own state? These crucial questions came during an age of colonialism, when Western powers viewed regions such as the Middle East, Africa, and Asia as being at their disposal. It was also then considered honorable to bring civilization to the native masses and to make good use of their natural resources.

It was not too long before European Jews got answers to their questions. Critical events such as the shocking Russian pogroms of 1881-1882 and the Dreyfus affair of 1894 convinced many Jews that it was impossible for them to become part of European society. The forces that were ultimately to result in modern Zionism were unleashed.

Arab Nationalism and World War I

At the same time that Jews were developing a national identity, Arabs were also beginning to express theirs. Arab nationalism, born of European ideas, was further reinforced by Arab hatred of Ottoman rule and a fear of a Jewish influx to Palestine. Palestinian nationalism, on the other hand, emerged later. Although Palestinians at first identified with the movement of

A Torah scroll; the Jewish claim to Palestine is rooted in history and in the Torah, the first five books of the Hebrew Bible. (Bill Aron/PhotoEdit)

Arab nationalism, it was not until the disintegration of the
Ottoman Empire in 1918 and the division of the Levant between
France and Great Britain that Palestinians began to develop a
separate national and political identity distinct from the rest of the
Arab people.

The Ottoman Empire had controlled the region known as
Palestine, and all Western Asia, from 1516 to its defeat by the
Allies in 1918. The region's population was also diverse, a result
of almost two thousand years of conquests and migrations. This
region was also desired by both France and Great Britain, who
for many years had been competing for a sphere of influence in
the Middle East. They both saw an opportunity to exert their
influence in the post-World War I period.

The Ottomans had entered the war on the side of the Germans
and thus had to be defeated. Meanwhile, Zionist leaders were
negotiating with Great Britain for a piece of land, and the British
government seemed to favor the idea of a Jewish homeland. In
1917, a British document known as the Balfour Declaration gave
Zionists a written guarantee of British support for the creation of
a Jewish home in Palestine. This document was a watershed in
the history of Zionism. In the Middle East, Arabs felt betrayed
since Great Britain had entered into previous agreements with
them (the Hussein-McMahon correspondence) that contradicted
the terms of the Balfour Declaration.

The Two World Wars and the Creation of Israel

When World War I ended, political boundaries had shifted,
new ones were created, and the Ottoman Empire crumbled,
leaving a power vacuum in the Middle East. After the war,
Palestine came under the British mandate — that is, British
administration of the region's political affairs. The following two
decades saw increasingly heightened tensions among all three
parties: the British, the Zionists, and the Palestinians.

These were also years of upheaval, whereby positions
constantly changed, attempts at solutions failed, brutal riots

between Zionists and Arabs erupted and were overlooked, and
Palestinian recommendations were ignored, not so much in
support of a Jewish state but because of European regional
interests.

The collective guilt felt over World War II and the near
extermination of European Jewry brought recognition that Jews
had to have a state in view of the persecution they had endured.
Unable to deal with the growing tensions between Arabs and
Zionists, Great Britain, in April, 1947, turned over the matter to
the United Nations, which voted in November of that same year
to partition Palestine into a Jewish state and an Arab state. The
United States was instrumental in pressing the United Nations to
create the Israeli state.

Following the proclamation of the Jewish state in 1948 and
after British withdrawal, most of the Arab countries attacked
Israel. After nine months of war, Israel emerged as a surprising
victor, resulting in the expansion of Israeli control of Palestine
and the occupation of the Gaza Strip by Egypt (1948-1967) and
the West Bank by Jordan (1948-1967). The Palestinians and their
Arab allies thus failed to maintain control of territories assigned
to them by the United Nations partition plan. One part of the
Palestinian population was dispersed to neighboring countries,
while the other part remained in Israel, the West Bank, and the
Gaza Strip.

Regional Conflicts

In the following years, Israel fought a number of regional wars.
The first war was the **1956 Suez War**, when Great Britain,
France, and Israel attacked Egypt as a result of a complex crisis
involving control of the Suez Canal, oil interests, weapons
supply, and past conflicts. The second war was the **June 1967
War**, which lasted only six days but was a turning point in Israeli
history. Following increasing regional tensions, in a preemptive
strike Israel defeated Egypt, Syria, and Jordan, gaining the

territories of the West Bank, the Gaza Strip, the Golan Heights, and the Sinai, as well as East Jerusalem. The third war was the **War of Attrition** (1968-1970), which was a protracted spillover of the 1967 war. The fourth war was the **October 1973 War**, also known as the Yom Kippur War, when Syria and Egypt attacked Israel in an effort to regain their territories. Israel might have been defeated had it not been for a massive American airlift. The fifth was the highly controversial **1982 Invasion of Lebanon**, which further destabilized the region, resulted in a shift in public opinion against Israel, and internationalized the Lebanese war. Nightly television broadcasts showing merciless Israeli shelling of Beirut, the Paris of the Mediterranean, brought international condemnation of Israel's actions in Lebanon as well as criticism from within Israel. After the invasion, many observers perceived Israel no longer as a tiny state surrounded by enemies but as the aggressor. Some critics of Israel took advantage of this change in perception to promote anti-Zionist attitudes. In some cases, criticism of Israel became a thinly veiled form of anti-Semitism.

The Role of the United States

The intensifying struggles for Palestinian and Israeli national identities and self-determination, as expressed in the post-1948 conflicts, increasingly drew global concerns and debates. In the 1950's, American policy as defined by the Eisenhower Administration was mainly to protect petroleum interests and to reduce Soviet influence in the Middle East, while at the same time maintaining good relations with Israel and the Arab states. Palestine and the Palestinians were not an issue at that time, which partially explains the failures of initial peace attempts.

Under President Kennedy, the United States began developing a "special relationship" with Israel, with high-tech weaponry and millions of dollars in aid going to the Jewish state. Following the 1967 Israeli victory over three Arab states, lobbying efforts on behalf of Israel intensified in Washington in order to increase all forms of support to the Jewish state. Washington, which at that time was bogged down in the Vietnam War, saw in Israel's sweeping 1967 victories a powerful, reliable, and strategic partner in the Middle East.

Under President Nixon and during Israel's War of Attrition, an American mediation plan for peace in the region was accepted, but Soviet and American regional rivalries continued to define the two world powers' strategies. During the 1970's, Secretary of State Henry Kissinger undertook diplomatic negotiations that ignored a short-term solution to the Israeli-Palestinian conflict but nevertheless resulted in the Sinai II Accord between Israel and Egypt, whereby Israel partially withdrew from the Sinai.

A new approach to the Israeli-Palestinian conflict was taken under President Jimmy Carter's Administration, when, for the first time, a need for a Palestinian homeland was stated as a requirement for peace in the Middle East. President Carter played a major mediating role between Egypt and Israel. In part as a result of intense distrust between Egypt's president Anwar Sadat and Syria's president Hafez Assad, in an unprecedented move President Sadat signed the Camp David Accords with Israel, paving the way for peace between the two states.

The Changing World Scene

The sweeping changes that occurred on the international scene in the late 1980's and early 1990's rendered the national interests that once shaped the policies of both the United States and the Soviet Union no longer valid. Events such as the warming of East-West relations, the collapse of the Soviet Union, the changing map of Eastern Europe, greater worldwide recognition of the PLO, the rise of the Intifada, the proliferation of weapons of mass destruction, the flow of Soviet Jews to Israel, and the Middle East peace negotiations will all have considerable repercussions on the Arab-Israeli conflict. These are some of the issues that concern not only Jewish Americans but the whole international community as well.

8 Is Anti-Semitism Still a Problem?

Because of their history, the Jews have learned to keep a watchful eye on anti-Semitic trends. Jewish organizations and think tanks, devoted to the defense of the Jewish people, monitor religious, political, social, and economic changes and attempt to analyze and predict their effects on Jews.

Various scholarly and authoritative yearly reports and monthly newsletters detail the state of anti-Semitism in the United States. Whether anti-Semitism is or is not a problem, Jews perceive anti-Semitism as an ever-looming potential problem, which has arisen too often in the past and recurred again and again in new forms.

Fears Persist Despite Jewish Success

Though the American Jewish Committee reported in January, 1992, that anti-Semitism is at an all-time low in the United States, the American-Jewish community is gripped by anxiety over its future. It is ironic that despite the unparalleled success and security Jews have achieved in the United States, they fear that other Americans may turn against Israel and, in the process, against Jewish Americans as well.

In 1992, there were eight Jewish senators and thirty-three Jewish Americans serving in the House of Representatives. Jews are now presidents of some of the most prestigious universities—

where not too long ago they were subjected to restrictive quotas. Also prominent in communications, law, the sciences, medicine, and other aspects of American culture, Jews are far out of proportion for their numbers in highly visible positions in the United States. They remember, however, that in the past their high visibility and success were used against them to make them scapegoats, and the threat of renewed anti-Semitism continues to worry the Jewish-American community today.

In fact, Jews in the early 1990's are more concerned about their situation than at any other time since World War II. Dramatic events in the early 1990's, and their effects on the relationship between the United States and Israel, have surprised everyone. Since the expulsion of Iraq from Kuwait in the 1991 Persian Gulf War, the United States has shifted to a more "even-handed" policy in the Middle East. In an attempt to encourage Arabs and Israelis to make peace, the United States has assumed the role of an "honest broker" prodding and coercing all parties as the slow-moving peace talks progress. This shift in policy concerns many American Jews.

Changing World Scene Troubles Jews

The United States, which emerged as the only real superpower after the economic collapse of the Soviet Union, entered a new era of friendship and cooperation with its former enemy. Under the leadership of President Bush and his emissary, Secretary of State James Baker III, the United States and the former USSR have called for a "new world order," where international disputes are solved peacefully in accordance with international law and goodwill. Since Israel's military power is no longer needed by the United States to offset a Soviet military threat in the Middle East, the alliance between the United States and Israel has lost strength.

What troubles American Jewry as well as Jews everywhere is precisely that change. Throughout their history, any change, even change that seemed best for everyone at the time, too often has not benefited the Jews. Though most Jews would certainly like to see the plight of the Palestinians resolved and the Arab-Israeli conflict settled, they fear that the creation of a Palestinian state next to Israel will pave the way toward the defeat and destruction of tiny Israel, alone in the vast Islamic world. Today, Israel is being asked to entrust its security to the "new world order," but this arrangement reminds Jews of many painful choices they have been forced to make throughout their bloody history, leaving them at the mercy of others.

Anti-Zionist propaganda emanating from the oil-rich Arab world and the former Soviet bloc has succeeded in changing the attitudes of many Americans toward Israel. Once seen as an underdog and a progressive nation that made the desert bloom, Israel is now often presented in the press and media as an aggressor nation in the region and in violation of Palestinian human rights. The American political Left, which for decades supported Zionist ideals, recently has become severely critical of Israel.

Anti-Zionism as the New Anti-Semitism

Anti-Zionism has emerged as the new, sophisticated anti-Semitism. This form of anti-Semitism must be distinguished from legitimate criticism of Israel, which does not deny Israel's right to exist or use criticism of specific Israeli policies as a pretext to attack Jewish people everywhere. The idea that Jewish people have no historical or spiritual claim in Palestine and therefore have no right of self-determination has gained popularity among anti-Semites worldwide. PLO Chairman Yasser Arafat has often stated that peace in the Middle East will only come with the destruction of Israel. Zionism, which in the past was associated with hope, freedom, and justice, has now become a dirty word in many circles, and its pejorative use can sometimes be heard on the evening news.

United Nations Resolution 3379, adopted in 1975, flatly stated that Zionism is a form of racism. Originally passed in a vote of the General Assembly, Resolution 3379 was orchestrated by Arab countries, the former Soviet bloc, and Third World nations in need of Arab oil money. Only in January, 1992, with the help of President George Bush, was this resolution revoked in the United Nations. Meanwhile, much damage has been done. The effect of the anti-Zionist campaign and the U.N. resolution has been that this new form of anti-Semitism entered into textbooks, and for fifteen years was taught in universities, schools, and countless other institutions. What concerns Jews is the lesson of German anti-Semitism, which was legitimized in German universities and ultimately allowed educated men and women to participate in the Holocaust.

Jewish students in American universities and colleges have been increasingly subjected to anti-Zionist propaganda and have been victimized by accusations that as Zionists they are racists by definition. Indoctrinated in anti-Zionism, Arab exchange students have used American universities as a platform to attack Israel's right to exist and have attempted to downgrade Jewish student organizations in full view of the student body. At California State University, San Francisco, Palestinian students have suggested that Jews should not be allowed to run for student government becaused they are Zionists and therefore racists. That Zionism, Jews, and Israel are all tainted with racism and evil was the intent and is the legacy of Resolution 3379.

Modern Views Are Reminders of Past

Though there is no organized anti-Semitic political movement in the United States, Pat Buchanan, the conservative columnist, well known for his anti-Israeli views, emerged in 1992 as a serious critic and challenger to President Bush from within Republican ranks. Buchanan's past remarks regarding Jews have put him under suspicion for being an anti-Semite. With the wide appeal of his views on other issues, however, he became one of the dominant personalities in the 1992 presidential campaign. It is Buchanan's isolationism that reminds American Jews of the 1930's, when the United States stood idle abandoning Europe's Jews. Moreover, the possibility that a candidate opposed to Jewish interests may become president on the merit of other issues haunts American Jewry.

The emergence of David Duke to national attention has surprised everyone and embarrassed the Republican Party. Duke, a former member of the American Nazi party and past leader of the Ku Klux Klan, lost his bid for governor of Louisiana to a collective sigh of relief in the American Jewish community. The fight against Duke succeeded in part because of a joint effort by ethnic and religious minorities. The defeat of Duke was a victory for coalition politics and may contribute in a small way to bridging the widening gap between Jews and blacks.

Jews and African Americans

The roots of the conflict between Jews and African Americans are complex. In the eyes of some blacks, Jewish landlords and owners of small businesses in black ghettos were profiting at the expense of blacks. Despite such resentment, Jewish organizations strongly supported the black struggle for equality, and Jewish voters traditionally supported candidates with a strong record on civil rights.

In the 1960's, however, tensions between Jews and blacks began to increase. During this time, some prominent Jewish leaders broke ranks with their fellow liberals, who had been reluctant to criticize the excesses of militant black activists such as the Black Panthers. Also, the growing influence of the Nation of Islam in the black community contributed to the worsening of relations between blacks and Jews.

After Israel's victories in the 1967 war and again in the Yom Kippur war of 1973, many African countries broke diplomatic relations with Israel, joining a Third-World bloc allied with Arab states. Following Africa's lead, some black leaders in the United States severed their relationship with American Jewry.

Affirmative action is another issue that has created tension between the two communities. Though many Jews support affirmative action, many also are wary of it because it encourages the use of quotas. Since quotas have been used so often in the past to discriminate against Jews, may Jews see the dangers even in well-intentioned quota-systems.

In the 1980's, some black leaders further distanced themselves from the Jewish-American community. In remarks that were not intended to be made public, Jesse Jackson, the most popular black politician and presidential candidate made derogatory references to Jews. Israel's controversial transfer of military technology to South Africa further aggravated relations between American Jews supportive of Israel and American blacks determined to end apartheid and white minority rule in South Africa. Clashes between black and Jewish college students sometimes escalated to bitter confrontations, while Nation of Islam leader Louis Farrakhan's outspoken anti-Semitism and anti-Zionism gained some acceptance in black America.

In 1991, violence against Jews erupted in the Crown Heights section of Brooklyn, New York, after an orthodox Hasidic Jew accidentally killed a young black boy in an automobile accident. A gang of angry black youths later stabbed to death another innocent Hasidic Jew in revenge. More violence flared up when bands of young blacks rampaged through the neighborhood stoning synagogues, Jewish homes, and attacking individuals on the streets. Shouts of "kill the Jews" were heard, reminding residents of what their grandparents told them about pogroms in Eastern Europe.

Prospects for the Twenty-first Century

Despite Jewish concerns over anti-Zionism and the shift in U.S. policy toward Israel, Jewish Americans are almost completely accepted as equals in the United States. That represents enormous progress. Yet new challenges face American Jews as they prepare to enter the twenty-first century. The incident in Crown Heights was only one of many recent scenes of racial and ethnic conflict. In both New York and Los Angeles, for example, tensions are high between the African-American community and the rapidly growing Korean-American community. As American society becomes increasingly diverse, the potential for conflict will also increase. In the multicultural society of the twenty-first century, Jewish Americans will be called on as they have been in the past not only to preserve the interests of their own community but also to play a leading role in ensuring tolerance and equal rights for all.

9 Some Who Made a Difference

In the first half of the twentieth century, anti-Semitism in democratic nations still remained a tremendous obstacle for Jews. Disappointed with the failures of democracies to live up to the principles they represented, a group of idealistic men and women of various backgrounds and persuasions emerged to address the hardships that Jews faced in the United States and abroad.

Although most of these individuals are now gone, their endeavors still live on. Their devotion to the causes they embraced helped shape the future of a people and provoked social, political, and religious change.

Louis D. Brandeis

Brandeis' distinguished contributions to both the American judicial system and Jewish nationalism made him a unique figure in American history. His emergence as a Zionist leader in 1914 revolutionized the movement in the United States and transformed it into a legitimate and potent force. His leadership not only restored American Jewry's sense of dignity but also gave hope to millions of Jews worldwide.

Born of Eastern European immigrant parents, in Louisville, Kentucky, on November 13, 1856, Brandeis grew up as an assimilated Jew, reared neither in Judaism nor in Christianity;

instead, his parents taught him concern for the "broader aspects of humanity."

After graduating from Harvard Law School with honors, Brandeis became a highly respected lawyer with his own private practice in Boston. Dubbed the "People's Attorney" because he often provided free legal advice to those in need, Brandeis battled for years not only for people's rights but also for the protection of society. He influenced the passage of several federal acts and published, among other things, *Other People's Money, and How the Bankers Use It* in 1914. In 1916, at the age of sixty, Brandeis was appointed by President Woodrow Wilson as an associate justice of the Supreme Court. The first Jew to hold this seat, Brandeis served on the Court for twenty-three years.

Brandeis came to the Jewish people as a secular American with an established reputation as a brilliant intellectual, a rationalist, and a determined reformer, but one who had little knowledge of the Jews and the Zionist struggle. As a youth, his parents had lost touch with Jewish matters, and, as an adult, he had rarely associated with Judaism, synagogues, or Zionists. Brandeis' leadership of the American Zionist movement was successful not because of his professional fame and seat on the Supreme Court — although these did lend the movement considerable prestige — but mainly because of his determination to reorganize the movement and his new interpretation of Zionism in relation to American patriotism and democracy.

Brandeis told American Jews that there was nothing wrong with being both a Zionist and an American, or having dual loyalty. The yearning for equality, liberty, and a homeland for the Jews represented a yearning for democracy, the United States' basic law. Therefore, to be a Zionist and to believe in those ideals was also to be a better American. Brandeis reinforced this by saying that the true loyalty of good citizens lies in their commitment to the profound values and principles their country stands for, and Jews should be proud to have such high goals in their struggle. These concepts coming from an eminent personality and a friend of President Woodrow Wilson made a

Louis D. Brandeis. (Library of Congress)

big difference to Jewish Americans and persuaded hundreds of thousands who were still undecided to embrace the Zionist cause. What Brandeis said was nothing new, but his unification of Zionism and Americanism was new.

Julian William Mack

Another notable leader of Jewish nationalism who also fought discrimination was Julian William Mack. Unlike Brandeis, who was ignorant of the Jewish world until late in life, Mack had always been active in the Jewish community of Chicago, where he worked and lived. However, it was not until 1914 that he became actively dedicated to Zionism.

Born July 19, 1866, in San Francisco, California, Mack was a lawyer, a university professor, a U.S. Circuit Court judge, an innovator in the juvenile court system, and a chairman of various national and federal organizations. In 1916, he added to his list of achievements the leadership of the Zionist organization.

Like Brandeis, Mack was attracted to the concept of Zionism because he believed that it was a well-founded and just cause and that Zionism did not clash with Americanism. The fact that American Jews supported the founding of a Jewish state did not make them "less good Americans." Mack believed that, just as German-Americans or Irish-Americans identified with their people, so Jewish-Americans could identify with their people and their ancestral homeland without diminishing their love for or loyalty to the United States. In 1918, Mack became instrumental in the reorganization of Zionism in the United States.

In 1922, his intervention against Harvard University's attempt to establish a "Jewish quota" opened the way to countless Jewish students. For many years, Mack had been a member of the Board of Overseers at Harvard University, a position that entailed the shaping of the institution's policies. When the president of Harvard University, A. Lawrence Lowell, asked Mack in 1922 to approve a proposal to restrict the number of Jewish students,

Mack was in a state of shock. To Lowell, the proposal seemed fair and beneficial to both Jewish students and others. To Mack, it was an assault on the Jews and a potential danger to their standing in the United States, especially coming from a prestigious institution such as Harvard University. Mack fought bitterly against the proposal, and it was eventually rejected.

Henrietta Szold

Few women in Jewish-American history showed as much compassion and devotion to a cause as did Henrietta Szold. Born in Baltimore, Maryland, on December 21, 1860, Szold is mostly remembered for her role in founding the Women's Zionist Organization of America, known as Hadassah, and her direction of Youth Aliyah, the organization that rescued tens of thousands of Jewish children from the grips of Nazi death camps and resettled them in Palestine.

Szold's commitment to help found Hadassah in 1912 resulted from her visit to Palestine a few years earlier, in 1909. The meager living conditions and shortage of medical care that she saw there made her resolve to take action. Hadassah not only provided trained nurses and health care but also sponsored youth camps and study groups. Hundreds of chapters of Hadassah sprouted throughout the United States with women of all ages joining.

In 1934, at the age of seventy-three, Szold undertook yet another humane project, transporting German-Jewish boys and girls threatened by Nazi terror to Palestine. Szold expanded the movement and played a major role in recommending the project to Hadassah, which in 1935 undertook the responsibility of sponsoring the project.

Reinhold Niebuhr

Among the Christians who made a difference in the struggle against anti-Semitism was Reinhold Niebuhr, a leading theologian

Henrietta Szold. (Jewish Historical Society of Maryland)

and political thinker of twentieth century America. Niebuhr's
intellectual concepts exerted considerable influence on religious,
political, and social thought.

Niebuhr began his career in 1915 as a pastor in Detroit and
later as a professor, before attracting national attention through
his publications and lectures. A Socialist in the 1930's and later a
Democrat, Niebuhr was at first opposed to war but changed his
stand with the rise of Hitler in Germany. Niebuhr was among the
first Christian theologians to perceive the dangers of Nazism to
Christianity as well as to the Jews.

The significance of Niebuhr in regards to American Jews lies
not only in the friendly relations he maintained with them during
a public and influential period of his career but also in the almost
unique efforts he undertook on their behalf, showing concern for
their future.

One of the main reasons Niebuhr urged American Christians
to support American intervention against Hitler was his
preoccupation with the fate of the Jews. His essay "Jews After
the War" not only attracted widespread attention but also made a
case for Zionism. For many years, Niebuhr was of the opinion
that it was not enough for Jews to have rights as individuals; they
deserved to have collective rights as a community, to maintain
their culture, tradition, and Jewish identity. For that reason,
Niebuhr believed Jews were entitled to a homeland and one in
Palestine.

Niebuhr acknowledged, however, that a home for the Jews in
Palestine would mean a violation of the sovereignty of the
Palestinians, and that no matter what the Western powers gave
the Arabs in return, it would be ridiculous to expect them to
regard a Jewish home in their midst as "just."

Niebuhr's concern as expressed in his speeches and writings
was enthusiastically received among leading Zionists. "Jews
After the War" was widely circulated among Zionist groups and
Niebuhr received hundreds of lecture invitations from Jewish
audiences. He was almost the only one to see a need to
reinterpret the church's relation to the Jews. After World War II,

Niebuhr continued his various social and political involvements, also becoming an adviser to the State Department.

Stephen Samuel Wise

Stephen Samuel Wise reached eminence as both a Reform rabbi and a Zionist leader and civic activist. Wise was born on March 17, 1874, in Budapest, Hungary; he was brought to the United States at the age of one, when his parents decided to leave the old country.

As a youth, Wise was not only fascinated with Judaism and politics but also had a voracious appetite for reading. He attended Columbia University, graduated with honors, and pursued rabbinical studies at the University of Oxford as well as in Vienna. In 1902, Wise earned a Doctor of Philosophy degree from Columbia University.

After beginning a rabbinical career in New York and then Portland, Oregon, where he was also active as a social worker, Wise returned to New York and in 1907 founded the Free Synagogue. Wise's theological principles differed sharply from those of most Reform rabbis of that day. Instead of devoting his sermons to theological issues, Wise addressed ethics and current social problems from his pulpit.

Wise's interest and involvement in current affairs and his deep love for his people and democracy made him among the very first Jewish Americans to be captured by the ideas of the Jewish National movement, or Zionism. Wise was present at the Second Zionist Congress held in 1898 in Basel, Switzerland, and there he met Theodor Herzl, the founder of modern Zionism.

Strongly influenced by Herzl's ideas, Wise, who was an eloquent speaker, became a founder of the Zionist Organization of America and was its president twice. His dedication, along with that of Louis D. Brandeis and Felix Frankfurter, helped secure the Balfour Declaration from the British and its approval by President Woodrow Wilson.

In the 1920's and 1930's, while it took most Jews years to be awakened to the threat of Hitlerism, Wise was among the first to see the danger looming on the horizon. As early as 1923, ten years before Hitler became chancellor of Germany, Wise was preoccupied with alerting his fellow Jews about the increase of anti-Semitism in Germany and its danger. Wise battled for the United States, for justice, for democracy, and for the rights of the Jewish people. He died on April 19, 1949, at the age of seventy-five.

Bayard Rustin

Among African-American leaders who were deeply concerned with anti-Semitism and race relations, including those between blacks and Jews, was Bayard Rustin. Widely known as the principal organizer of the 1963 civil rights march on Washington and the school boycott in New York City in 1964, Rustin struggled for more than four decades for the rights of oppressed minorities in the world.

Born in West Chester, Pennsylvania, on March 17, 1912, Rustin was a civil rights activist, who followed the philosophy of Mahatma Ghandi and sought nonviolent solutions to human problems. Rustin's antiwar stand during World War II caused him to be sentenced to more than two years in prison as a conscientious objector. In the 1950's and 1960's, Rustin devoted his time and energy to pacifist organizations such as the Fellowship of Reconciliation and the War Resisters League, of which Albert Einstein was honorary chairman. He also worked for Martin Luther King, Jr. and was the executive director of the A. Philip Randolph Institute and its cochairman for many years.

Throughout his career, Rustin fiercely denounced the stereotyping and the fantasies with which bigots characterized both blacks and Jews. For many years, Rustin was also troubled by the deteriorating relations between blacks and Jews, especially in city ghettos such as Harlem. He deplored the anti-Semitic trends that he saw gaining strength among the poor and the uneducated, feeling that it would be "one of the great tragedies" for black and Jews one day to become prejudiced and discriminate against each other.

Rustin urged his people to fight the increasing hostilities and warned black communities not to join in "history's oldest and most shameful witch hunt, anti-Semitism," calling such pursuit an act of "self-destruction" and an unwise detractor from the "real oppressor."

Franklin H. Littell

A religious educator who has tackled the thorny issue of Christian anti-Semitism is Franklin H. Littell, a Christian whose thought-provoking concepts have challenged traditional and contemporary Christian thought.

Littell was born in Syracuse, New York, on June 20, 1917. He was educated at Cornell College, Union Theological Seminary, and Yale University, where he received his Ph.D. in 1946. He was the chief protestant adviser to the U.S. High Commissioner in Germany. He has taught at numerous institutions and is the author of many books, including *The German Church Struggle and the Holocaust* (1974), *The Crucifixion of the Jews* (1975), and *The Macmillan Atlas History of Christianity* (1976).

Littell has explained that the basis of Christian anti-Semitism is the Christian attitude or "superseding myth" that sees the role of the Jewish people to have ended with the arrival of Jesus Christ. Such a belief, he says, suggests murder, since it teaches that "a people's mission in God's providence is finished, that they have been relegated to the limbo of history." The re-creation of Israel, however, refutes this traditional myth, and Littell sees this as posing an immense challenge to modern Christian theology.

Littell explains that the Holocaust, or the murder of six million Jews during World War II, was carried out by baptized Christians "from whom membership in good standing was not (and has not yet been) withdrawn, rai[sing] the most insistent question about the credibility of Christianity."

Littell sees an indispensable need for a redefinition of the relationship between Christians and Jews and asks of those who call themselves Christians to come to grips with their religious anti-Semitism, past and present. He says that Christians must acknowledge their guilt and repent, instead of isolating the Holocaust as a purely German affair, an aberration, and exonerating church leaders who could have done something but did not. Littell noted that what is most frightening is that most Christian institutions still do not take the Holocaust seriously. This concern, which Littell had expressed in the 1970's in his book *The Crucifixion of the Jews*, can be seen exemplified in the early 1990's by the Catholic church: More than forty years after the establishment of the state of Israel, the Vatican still has not recognized Israel's sovereignty.

10 Time Line

1950 B.C.	In the biblical account, Abraham, the founder of the Hebrew nation and the Jewish religion, establishes a special relationship with God in Israel.
1250 B.C.	Moses, the lawgiver, leads the children of Israel out of slavery in Egypt.
725 B.C.	The Assyrians invade and, in the process, destroy ten of the twelve original tribes of Israel.
597 B.C.	Jerusalem falls and the Israelites are deported to Babylon but return to Israel fifty years later.
332 B.C.	Alexander the Great defeats the Persian Empire, invading Asia, and Israel is occupied in the process.
63 B.C.	The Roman Empire replaces the Greeks, who ruled the Jewish people, continuing centuries of occupation.
32 A.D.	Jesus of Nazareth is crucified, setting the stage for the emergence of Christianity.
66-70 A.D.	The first great Jewish uprising against Rome ends in disaster and marks the beginning of the expulsion of Jews from Palestine by the Romans.
570 A.D.	Mohammed, the founder of Islam, is born in what is today Saudi Arabia.
1095	The beginning of the Crusades to free the Holy Land from Islam also stimulates anti-Semitism in Christian Europe.
1492	Jews are forced out of Spain during the Spanish Inquisition.
1516-1918	The Ottoman (Turkish) Empire neglects the Middle East for more than four hundred years.
1881-1903	Pogroms in Czarist Russia cause the first wave of Jewish immigration to Palestine.
1897	The first Zionist Congress meets and affirms the need to reestablish a homeland for the Jewish people.
1917	The Balfour Declaration states that Great Britain favors the establishment of a Jewish homeland in Palestine.
1929	Tension and violence between Arabs and Zionists increase in Palestine.

1936-1939	Great Britain puts down an Arab rebellion and expells Palestinian leaders.
1939	Great Britain restricts Jewish immigration to Palestine as World War II begins and the situation of European Jewry becomes desperate.
1947	Great Britain requests the United Nations to settle the question of a Jewish homeland, resulting in the creation of Israel in a vote of the General Assembly.
1948	Arab states attack Israel one day after Israel is proclaimed a sovereign state.
1956	Britain, France, and Israel attack Egypt after Abdel Nasser, the Egyptian leader, nationalizes the Suez Canal.
1967	While Egypt, Jordan, and Syria prepare for attack, Israel strikes first, resulting in an overwhelming victory, leaving the Sinai, Gaza, West Bank, and Golan Heights under Israeli control.
1973	Egypt and Syria strike back at Israel in an attempt to regain lost territory and Arab pride in the Yom Kippur surprise attack.
1979	Israeli-Egyptian peace treaty negotiated with the help of President Jimmy Carter is signed in Washington.
1981	The Israeli Air Force in a daring raid bombs an Iraqi nuclear reactor but is condemned by the Security Council of the United Nations.
1982	Israel invades Lebanon in an attempt to secure its Northern border from PLO terrorist attacks.
1987	The Intifada, a Palestinian revolt in the West Bank and Gaza Strip, begins.
1991	Iraq is defeated by American and coalition forces, while Israel watches on the sidelines but is nevertheless hit by Iraqi Scud missiles.
1991-1992	President George Bush initiates peace talks between Arabs and Israelis as well as Israelis and Palestinians to resolve the Middle East conflict.

11 Bibliography

Bin Talal, Hassan. *Palestinian Self-Determination: A Study of the West Bank and Gaza Strip*. New York: Quartet Books, 1981. Written by the Crown Prince of Jordan and the youngest brother of King Hussein of Jordan. Explores the historical background and the legal issues and claims. Appendices.

Clayton-Felt, Josh. *To Be Seventeen in Israel: Through the Eyes of an American Teenager*. New York: Franklin Watts, 1987. Written by Josh when he was seventeen and aimed at teenage readers. Josh went to Israel to find out how teenagers live in that part of the world surrounded by daily tensions. Photographs, index.

Dolan, Edward F., Jr. *Anti-Semitism*. New York: Franklin Watts, 1985. For younger readers, this book provides a clear and concise explanation of the causes of anti-Semitism, anti-Zionism, and prejudice. Also contains a chapter on the Holocaust, a list of further readings, and an index.

Frangi, Abdallah. *The PLO and Palestine*. London: Zed Books, 1982. Provides a Palestinian perspective on the Palestinian-Israeli conflict. The author is a Palestinian and a member of the Al-Fateh Revolutionary Council. Maps, guide to further reading, and charts on the structure of the PLO.

Elazar, Daniel J. *Communitity Polity: The Organizational Dynamics of American Jewry*. Philadelphia: The Jewish Publication Society of America, 1976. A comprehensive analysis of the organized Jewish community in the United States. Surveys the history, structure, problems, and future outlook.

Gerber, David A., ed. *Anti-Semitism in American History*. Chicago: University of Illinois Press, 1986. A Collection of thirteen essays by fourteen authors. Explores specific topics such as anti-Semitism in the State Department and in universities, the stereotyping of Jews, and the demagogues of anti-Semitism.

Gerner, Deborah J. *One Land, Two People: The Conflict Over Palestine*. San Francisco: Westview Press, 1991. This book in the Dilemmas in World Politics series is an excellent introduction to the Israeli-Arab conflict, examining both sides. Notes, chronology, glossary, index, and more.

Gilbert, Martin. *The Holocaust: A History of the Jews of Europe During the Second World War*. New York: Holt, Rinehart and Winston, 1985. The definitive account on the Holocaust. Essential reading for anyone trying to comprehend this outrageous crime. Draws heavily on testimonies of Holocaust survivors.

Hertzberg, Arthur. *The Jews in America: Four Centuries of Uneasy Encounter*. New York: Simon & Schuster, 1989. This fine contribution to the history of the Jews starts with the arrival in 1654 of a few Jews in New Amsterdam, traces the Jewish experience throughout the centuries, and ends with the 1980's. Index.

Johnson, Paul. *A History of the Jews*. New York: Harper & Row, 1987. A comprehensive history of the Jews from antiquity to the present. Johnson presents an insightful study that is excellently researched and well written. Epilogue, glossary, source notes, index.

Kamin, Josephine. *The Hebrew People: A History of the Jew*. New York: McGraw-Hill, 1968. For juvenile readers. Traces the rise of anti-Semitism as a result of social, political, economic, and religious pressures. A compassionate and absorbing account of the Hebrews, beginning in 331 B.C. Illustration, photographs.

Marrow, Alfred J. *Changing Patterns of Prejudice: A New Look at Today's Racial, Religious, and Cultural Tensions*. New York: Chilton, 1962. Although dated, this volume contains a good chapter, "Patterns of Prejudice," on the origins of prejudice, its spread, and manifestations. Appendices, index.

Perl, William R. *The Holocaust Conspiracy: An International Policy of Genocide*. New York: Shapolsky Publishers, 1989. Provides extensively documented answers to critical questions. Some notable chapters are "Conspiracy in the American Hierarchy," "How the Allies kept Auschwitz Operating," and "The Moral Powers." Foreword by Senator Claiborne Pell. Glossary, epilogue, index.

Prager, Dennis, and Joseph Telushkin. *Why the Jews? The Reasons for Antisemitism*. Simon & Schuster, 1983. This thought-provoking book examines various historical aspects of anti-Semitism, including Christian, Islamic, Leftist, Nazi, and anti-Zionist. Essential reading. Notes, bibliography of cited works, index.

Viorst, Milton. *Sands of Sorrow: Israel's Journey from Independence*. New York: Harper & Row, 1987. Gives an even-handed insight into the Arab-Israeli conflict and the Palestinian-Israeli conflict. Explains the role of world powers in the Middle East. Appendices, select bibliography, index, maps.

Wyman S. David. *The Abandonment of the Jews: America and the Holocaust, 1941-1945*. New York: Pantheon Books, 1984. This highly well-researched volume makes some stunning and troubling revelations, shedding new light on the Holocaust controversy. Wyman, a Christian Protestant of Swedish descent, explores the reasons why Jews were not rescued until too late. Essential reading.

Yaseen, Leonard C. *The Jesus Connection: To Triumph Over Anti-Semitism.* New York: Crossroads, 1985. A moving, enlightening, and easy-to-read book. Particularly interesting to younger readers is the chapter "The Jewish Connection," featuring photographs and brief biographies of famous and less than famous Jews. Introduction by Evangelist Billy Graham.

12 Media Materials

The Arab-Israeli Conflict (1974; 16mm). This objective examination outlines the history of the region, explains Great Britain's role in shaping it, analyzes the political and territorial problems (West Bank, Gaza Strip, Golan Heights, and Jerusalem), and considers a few solutions for peace.

Children of Abraham (1968; 16mm). Starts with the beginning of Judaism and discusses the Torah, Talmud, and Jewish laws and rituals. Also examines the major branches of Judaism in Israel and the United States.

From Dust and Ashes: Survivors, Scholars, and Clergy Confront the Holocaust (1983; 16mm). Documents and analyzes through personal accounts and recollections as well as through historical photographs the attempt to annihilate Europe's Jews during World War II. Describes the starvation, isolation, fright, and inhuman treatment that Jews faced in the ghettos and concentration camps. Scholars and clergy examine the tragedy and the world's reaction to it, both in the past and in the present.

Jewish Americans. A touching narrative that portrays the Jewish experience in the United States. Through historical photographs, this film depicts the persecution and discrimination Jews encountered, then relates the story of the Jewish East Side.

The Legacy: Children of Holocaust Survivors (1979; 16mm). Through interviews with adult offspring of Holocaust survivors, this film relates the impact of the event on their lives and how they live with a continuous fear. Also discusses common characteristics among survivors.

Prejudice: Perceiving and Believing (1977; 16mm). Explores the causes of prejudice and shows that it is not based on reality but on prejudgment. Examines its irrationality and destructive consequences.

Who Are the American Jews? (1972; 16mm). Documents the life of Jews in the United States, beginning with the arrival in 1654 (have to check date) of twenty-three Portuguese Jews. Follows the evolution of American Jews through the centuries, with a focus on Judaism, Jewish culture, and Jewish qualities and life-style.

13 Resources

American Jewish Congress
15 E. 84th Street
New York, NY 10028
(212) 879-4500

Founded in 1918, this association is composed of Jewish Americans who disapprove of racism and are dedicated to the unity, dignity, and survival of Jews everywhere. Grants awards, maintains library, and publishes journals and newsletters, including *The American Jewish Congress — National Report*. Also sponsors Institute for Jewish-Christian Relations.

American Jewish Committee
c/o Institute of Human Relations
165 E. 56th Street
New York, NY 10022
(212) 751-4000

Established in 1906, the AJC organizes programs on research, education, human relations, and works to fight bigotry and protect religious and civil rights. Maintains a library and publishes the quarterly *AJC Journal*. In conjunction with the Jewish Publication Society, the AJC also publishes the *American Jewish Year Book*, an invaluable annual survey of events and trends of interest to Jews throughout the world.

American Jewish Joint Distribution Committee
711 3rd Avenue
New York, NY 10017
(212) 687-6200

This organization, created in 1914, provides health, welfare, and relief assistance, as well as programs to rehabilitate needy Jews in several continents. Publishes *American Jewish Joint Distribution Committee — Annual Report*. Also offers a wide range of programs, funds, training, and services.

Anti-Defamation League of B'nai B'rith
823 United Nations Plaza
New York, NY 10017
(212) 490-2525
   The ADL, established in 1913, seeks to "stop the defamation of Jewish people and to secure justice and fair treatment to all citizens." Also aims to fight anti-Semitism and anti-democratic extremism. Maintains the International Center for Holocaust Studies and the Jewish Foundation for Christian Rescuers, among others. Bestows awards, sponsors literary competitions, and publishes several journals and newsletters, including the *Anti-Defamation League Bulletin*.

Council of Jewish Federations
730 Broadway
New York, NY 10003
(212) 475-5000
   Created in 1932, this organization raises funds for national and international Jewish needs through an association of local federations, welfare funds, and community councils. Maintains a library and publishes the biennial *Council Publication* and the annual *Federation Directory, among others*.

Hadassah, The Women's Zionist Organization of America
50 W. 58th Street
New York, NY 10019
(212) 355-7900
   Founded in 1912, this organization of more than 380 thousand members carries out numerous community services and programs in the United States and Israel. Operates Hadassah University Hospital and the Hadassah Hebrew University Medical Center, both in Israel. Supports Youth Aliyah. Maintains a 4,000-volume library; among its many publications are *Hadassah Magazine* and *The American Scene*.

National Conference of Christians and Jews
71 5th Avenue, Suite 1100
New York, NY 10003-3095
(212) 206-0006
   Created in 1928, this organization promotes better human relations and is composed of people of all religions. Encourages toleration through education and studies all forms of prejudice. Conducts various programs, training, and workshops. Bestows awards and maintains a publications department.

National Jewish Community Relations Advisory Council
433 Park Avenue South
New York, NY 10016
(212) 684-6950

Founded in 1944, this association works with other agencies to develop policies to fight anti-Semitism and the oppression of Jews and to protect civil rights, religious freedom, and democratic principles. Publishes *Directory of Constituent Organizations.*

United Jewish Appeal — Federation of Jewish Philanthropies of New York
130 E. 59th Street
New York, N.Y. 10022
(212) 980-1000

Founded in 1986, and operating with a budget of 30 million dollars, this organization provides a broad range of services, including medical, vocational, and child care. Some of its many departments are Housing and Neighborhood Preservation, Human Services, Policy Research and Planning, and Public and Community Affairs. Maintains biographical archives and grants several awards.

DISCRIMINATION

JEWISH AMERICANS
STRUGGLE FOR
EQUALITY

INDEX